Noticing the Divine

An Introduction to Interfaith Spiritual Guidance

JOHN R. MABRY

GW00676351

MOREHOUSE PUBLISHING

HARRISBURG — NEW YORK

This book is dedicated to
GINA ROSE HALPERN,
who asked me to teach.

Portions of chapter 2 ("Taoism and Nondirection") adapted from *God As Nature Sees God* by John R. Mabry (Element Books, 1994/Apocryphile Press, 2004); "The Way of Non-Direction," *Presence* (June 1998); *God Has One Eye* by John R. Mabry (Apocryphile Press, 2006). All rights held by the author and used here by permission.

Portions of chapters 3, 4, and 5 adapted from *God Has One Eye* by John R. Mabry (Apocryphile Press, 2006). All rights held by the author and used here by permission.

Portions of chapter 9 ("Sikhism and the Interfaith Path") adapted from "Three Modes of Interfaith Direction" (*Presence*, June 2004). All rights held by the author and used here by permission

Morehouse Publishing, P.O. Box 1321, Harrisburg, PA 17105

Morehouse Publishing, 445 Fifth Avenue, New York, NY 10016

Morehouse Publishing is an imprint of Church Publishing Incorporated.

Cover design by Brenda Klinger

Library of Congress Cataloging-in-Publication Data
Mabry, John R.
 Noticing the divine : an introduction to interfaith spiritual guidance / by John R. Mabry.
   p. cm.
 Includes bibliographical references (p.   ).
 ISBN-13: 978-0-8192-2238-1 (pbk.)
 1. Spiritual direction. 2. Religious pluralism. I. Title.
BL624.M275 2006
206'.1—dc22
                2006029568
Printed in the United States of America
06 07 08 09   10 9 8 7 6 5 4 3 2 1

Contents

Introduction

"You have got to be kidding." That was the first thing my students said when I opened up discussion on our reading for the month. It was the second session of our Introduction to Spiritual Guidance class, and I had assigned a chapter from that long-revered and predictably required textbook, *The Practice of Spiritual Direction* by William A. Barry and William J. Connolly.

"Okay," I told them, "I knew this book was going to require some internal translation as you went along—" "Translation?" Another student piped up. "This doesn't require 'translation,' it's from an alien paradigm. 'Internal givenness to the Lord'? What the hell does that mean? Who talks like that? And besides, I'm Jewish, and this book is insulting."

"And I'm Buddhist," said another student. "This book makes no sense to me whatsoever, because I don't believe in God."

"*Oy vey,*" I said to myself. All of the students were adamant. They did *not* like this book. It did not speak their language—its instructions were written in a form of Catholicese that was utterly obscure to most of them, and the religious assumptions of the text did not speak to the lived experience of any of them. There was one woman who was an ex-Catholic, and while she understood the language, it made her angry.

It very quickly became clear to me that this textbook was not going to fly in an interfaith seminary like the Chaplaincy Institute for Arts and Interfaith Ministry. This realization started me out on a search for an interfaith textbook that could address the real needs of my students. And while there was one book out there claiming to be *"The Complete Guide to Interfaith Spiritual Direction,"* it was clearly written for the layperson seeking to receive spiritual direction; it was not a textbook for those learning to *be* spiritual directors.

I realized that I would have to write my own textbook if my students were to have something appropriate for them. By the time the next group of students rolled through the program, I was ready. Staying one month ahead of them for the better part of a year, this book was born.

An Interfaith Approach

In times past, spiritual guidance was given within a specific religious community. Jews went to their rabbis (teachers) for guidance, Catholics sought direction from other Catholics, etc. This was the way things had always been done, and it had worked for centuries. But the world was changing. About forty years ago, a shift occurred in Roman Catholic training programs for spiritual directors. Laypeople had discovered the ministry, and started coming to be trained. Progressive Catholics encouraged a ministry open to the laity, and the ranks of the training programs began to swell. Then about twenty-five years ago, another unforeseen shift occurred: Protestant Christians, who had sought direction from Catholic spiritual guides, came themselves to be trained. This took a little more accommodation, but it soon became commonplace to have Catholics and Protestants learning the art of spiritual guidance side-by-side. But the surprises just kept coming: about ten years ago, Jews and Buddhists started showing up and asking to be trained. And so long as they did not mind being trained according to a Christian model, many programs learned to accommodate them, too.

The ministry has continued to spread across religious boundaries. Interfaith spiritual guidance is no longer an aberration, it is the norm for most of us who practice the art, regardless of how we were trained. For those in training now, the current curriculum cannot completely meet their needs, since our training materials have yet to catch up with the reality lived by most of us in the field. This book is one attempt to meet this growing need.

The first portion of each chapter is an introduction to a different world religion. I felt this was important; while my students come from a variety of religious backgrounds, many of them have only a limited exposure to faiths other than the ones they themselves practice. This has to be addressed in training because one never knows who is going to step through that door. Will it be a Hindu? Might he or she be an atheist or Jewish or Wiccan? To be properly prepared for the task, I knew my students would need to have a good grounding in the world's religions so that they would feel comfortable and prepared no matter *who* stepped through their doors. Outside reading was assigned to give them more in-depth exposure to each tradition, as well.

As I reflected upon each of the world's traditions, it struck me that although every religion addressed the same needs—people are people, regardless of where you go, after all—each one was also distinctive, emphasizing differing aspects of the spiritual life, and possessed unique light to shed on the spiritual guidance process. Gradually it occurred to me that all traditions had something specific to teach us about the ministry due to their diverse emphases. No doubt one could find each piece in any tradition if one looked hard enough, but there, on the surface, clear for anyone willing to see was one thing vital to the ministry that each tradition has to teach, and teaches so well. Thus, the mythology of native traditions teaches us the value of telling our sacred stories; Taoism teaches us the importance of "not doing," learning to trust the Divine as the real spiritual guide; Judaism teaches us about the law and how to honor appropriate boundaries in our ministries, etc. We can honor every tradition equally, but each religion has a special gift to bestow on those who are learning the art.

Nomenclature

While writing this book, I have been keenly aware that some of the terminology in vogue in the spiritual direction community was going to be problematic for my students—some of it is problematic to the spiritual direction community itself. I understand that people will take issue with some of the choices I have made. So be it. They were made carefully and prayerfully with the needs of my immediate students in mind, and after having taught the material for a year I am confident that they were the right choices. That said, they may not be right for everyone in every program, and like almost every book out there, it may require some internal translation. It worked for my students, but as my friend Liz Stout is fond of saying, "Your mileage may vary."

The first decision I made was in how to describe the ministry. Most people are familiar with the term "spiritual direction," yet this description is a misnomer. To say "I do spiritual direction" implies that I know what I am doing, that I am "directing" someone, that there is a hierarchical arrangement in which I am perceived to be somehow "superior." Yet none of this is true in my ministry. In ages past, when Zen students sat at the feet of the roshi, or Roman Catholics went to confession, the hierarchy was taken for granted. But this is no longer the case, and does not reflect the egalitarian theology most of us have come to embrace—nor does it acknowledge the deep impact that Rogerian psychotherapy has had in our understanding of the seeker as expert on his or her own spiritual life. Most people I know in the spiritual direction community chafe at the phrase "spiritual direction," and wish we could reach consensus on another that more accurately describes the contemporary reality. Many people prefer "soul friend," or "spiritual companion," or even "spiritual coach" to describe themselves, but when we want to talk about the ministry itself, we almost always revert to saying "spiritual direction," because that is the terminology everyone understands.

For this book, I have chosen to use the phrase "spiritual guidance," although this term is not without its own set of problems. It can still imply a hierarchy—after all, it is assumed that the director is "guiding," but it does not contain the "directive" baggage that many of us have come to associate with old-school forms of the ministry that are often holdovers from when it was conflated with confession in Roman Catholic practice.

This decision, of necessity, leads to other descriptive innovations. If we are learning "spiritual guidance" rather than "spiritual direction," then what do we call the one giving guidance, and the one receiving it? This book refers to those doing the guiding as "spiritual guides," which is not a big leap. What to call the "directee" is more problematic.

"Directee" has always been an inelegant term at best, and it has always stuck in my throat, because it is part of a proprietary vocabulary indecipherable to anyone not steeped in the ministry. Many of our own "directees" would likely wrinkle their noses to be called such. In this book I have exchanged the cliquish "directee" for the more conventional "client," borrowing from the lexicons of business, mental health, and the helping professions with which most people are familiar.

I realize this will be a controversial choice in some circles. There are many who lament the creeping "professionalization" of the ministry of spiritual guidance. They feel very strongly that the ministry is a charism given by God, not a skill one can learn. Some even feel that it is wrong to charge for their time.

Everyone is entitled to his or her opinions. Mine are: spiritual guidance is both a gift and a skill, and native talent and responsible training combine to create effective spiritual guides. In a ministry that is proliferating so quickly, I believe a set of professional standards of conduct that are generally agreed upon is imperative (a great debt is owed to Spiritual Directors International for supplying us with just such a document in their *Guidelines for Ethical Conduct*, reprinted in appendix A).

Economic realities face myself and most of my students. Very few of us have independent means of support; we have neither the leisure nor the wealth to approach our ministries as purely philanthropic endeavors or as a spiritual "hobby." Most of us today must work more than one job to make ends meet, and for those of us who feel a true calling to the ministry of spiritual guidance, this endeavor must contribute to our financial survival or we cannot responsibly devote such a large part of our time to it. It is not a hobby for most of us, it is a ministry. And, whether you like to think so or not, ministry is a profession that requires hard work, rigorous (and expensive) training, and strict standards of professional conduct.

The term "directee" comes with a bit of a clean slate for most of us, but the term "client" is loaded with all kinds of meanings, most of which will serve us. A client has rights, expects a certain standard of professionalism and care, has recourse in case of injury, and, of course, the client is always *right*. Nobody is quite sure what a directee can expect.

Finally, there is the matter of simple intelligibility. Outside of the current spiritual direction community, nobody knows what "directee" means. Everyone knows what a "client" is, even in reference to this ministry, and even if you don't like the term. And for people who are new to the ministry, it is instantly comprehensible—there is no need to induct them into some elite club with proprietary vocabularies or secret handshakes. Feel free to quibble, but for the purposes of this book, "client" is the preferred term.

Now that we have the spiritual guide and the client sorted out, what do we call the transcendent reality to which we are trying to help people orient their lives? Should I use a rotating set of terms, such as God,

Brahma, Buddha Nature, Allah, the Tao, the Goddess, the *Èlan vital*, and the Universe? I toyed with the idea, but I feared such a kaleidoscopic approach would prove disorienting and fragmented. There is one transcendent reality, I assume, that all of our religions address according to their own traditions, and using a variety of names would obscure the unity of purpose I was aiming for. Instead I decided to use the term "Divinity" or "the Divine" to describe the ultimate reality and its infinite faces.

This, of course, comes with its own set of problems. First, the term is as incomprehensible as "God" to many atheists, agnostics, and humanists. I regret I have not been able to find a word or name that can adequately reference transcendent reality while taking into account those who deny the possibility of a transcendent reality. No doubt this is through my own fault, a lack of imagination perhaps, but I suspect it is also due to the limitations of language. I have simply not been able to find a word in the English language that works better.

Another problem with "the Divine" is that it seems to describe a thing—perhaps a process or a principle—rather than a person. This is very attractive to some people, but it will leave others cold. An advantage to this is that a *thing* is, in English, gender-neutral, while *people* are necessarily gendered. Since my students are keenly sensitive to gender issues, a gender-neutral term for transcendent reality was an imperative for this book. Again, there is simply not another word in the English language that can pull as much weight—with fewer limitations—than "Divinity." It's not perfect, but it is arguable whether Divinity is, either!

Deep Ecumenism

An overarching assumption in this book is that no religious tradition is superior to any other. Every tradition is a valid and valuable expression of the Divine, couched in the cultural language and symbols of a certain people in a particular place and time. The Divine is Divinity no matter where you find it, but the cultural clothes in which Divinity is dressed are, to some extent, arbitrary. This is not to say that these arbitrary clothes are not beautiful, profound, soulful, or instructive. They are all of that, and more. They are unique, wise, relevant, grounded in the earth and human culture, and doubtless have great sentimental value for both adherents and sympathetic lookers-on. But every tradition also possesses its share of injustice, misogyny, prejudice, intolerance, and other evils. To ignore this reality and pretend otherwise is not honest.

This book does not take a critical approach, yet neither does it exalt, idolize, or otherwise revere any particular expression of the Divine. They are all flawed, and they are all fabulous. They are all worthy expressions of spiritual life, and valuable guides on the journey. Every person must decide for him- or herself what sources of spiritual wisdom make sense to him or her, and we cannot effectively guide them if we allow our own prejudices to influence our guidance. This is no small feat. Nevertheless, it is what is required of us if we are to be truly interfaith spiritual guides. We must neither demonize nor romanticize religious traditions when we sit with our clients. This book, likewise, seeks to do neither.

This is not a finished product. It is, instead, a first step. This book cannot, by itself, suffice to teach someone all the vagaries of the art of spiritual guidance. There can be no substitute for classroom instruction, and the importance of supplemental textual materials is taken for granted. I do hope that this book can, as its title suggests, serve as a basic introduction to the ministry as it is practiced in an interfaith context. To my knowledge, it is the first textbook on spiritual guidance written from a specifically interfaith approach. It is not perfect, it is not complete, and, no doubt, it is not always accurate. It is, however, the best I could do with the tools at hand, and for my students, it has proven useful. I pray you will find it of use, as well.

1

Native Traditions
and Storytelling

According to the Popol Vuh, the sacred memory of the Native American Mayans, the world began in suspense. All was calm, all was silent; the sky was empty, the sea was still; and time was pregnant, waiting for something to happen.

Floating in the water were the grandfathers: the makers, Tepeu and Gucumatz, who covered themselves in blue feathers and were surrounded by light. In the darkness of the night, Tepeu and Gucumatz began to talk to one another. They talked for a long time, and with their conversation they summoned the gods, which they called the Heart of Heaven.

The gods of lightening and thunder emerged from their words, and other gods also. Then the grandfathers spoke some more, and the world took form. Waters receded, dry ground appeared, and a great light appeared in the sky. Yet they were not satisfied, for the grandfathers desired human beings to care for the new world and to converse with them.

Their conversation brought forth the animals, but they could only squawk and howl. They could not invoke the Heart of Heaven and could not praise the grandfathers. "They cannot even say our names," they said to one another, "this will not do."

So the grandfathers fashioned human beings out of mud, but their creations washed away in the rains. So they tried again, but this time they consulted the grandmothers, who were great soothsayers. "Try making them out of plants," they said. So the grandfathers made human beings out of wood and corn, but the people they made had short memories and did not commune with the Heart of Heaven. So they smashed the wooden people and tried again.

The grandfathers spoke all night, and finally they formed human beings out of the food they would eat: cornmeal and dough and various tasty drinks. But they were not made, they were not born—they emerged from the talking of the grandfathers.

When the new people stood up, they praised the grandfathers, and they spoke about all the things they saw. But the grandfathers were dismayed, saying, "The new people see everything, they are just like us. Let's take them down a notch or two so that they do not become too powerful and become gods themselves." So the grandfathers blew mist into their eyes so that they could only see things that were near to them.

Since they were now shortsighted and could only see what was directly in front of them, the people depended on the grandfathers. They sacrificed to them, prayed to them, and through their words, they, too, sought to summon the Heart of Heaven.

Things are not so different now. For us, as for the ancient Mayans, it is still through the conversation of two friends that the Divine is summoned. It is through the sharing of desires and dreams, ambitions and fears that the gods come near, and new worlds come into being.

We may not float in water or cover ourselves with blue feathers, yet the ministry of spiritual guidance takes many forms, some of them strange. But in every method employed, there is something in common. People of sincere spirit meet and speak to one another about their relationships to the Divine. If we are faithful and fortunate, some of the mist clears from our eyes, and we see a bit more of the path than we did before.

Yet long before there were professional spiritual guides, before there were clients, before there were discernment groups or Ignatian retreats, before there were training programs or students or certificates, our ancestors gathered around the fire, telling their sacred stories about themselves and their gods. In the flicker of the flames, the Heart of Heaven came near to them, and together they discovered who they were, what was required of them, how to treat one another, and how they were related to the wild world around them.

All Creatures Are Kindred

The stories our ancestors told around their campfires revealed many amazing truths, but one of the most poignant for us today is the inherent relatedness of all beings. Our ancestors saw the world as being of one piece: the plants, the animals, the people, the land, the gods, and the seasons. All were part of one world, all were neighbors and relations. Humans belonged to the land as much as the yak or the beaver did. No one knows exactly when we humans were bitten by the arrogance bug, which made us believe that we were somehow distinct from, or superior to nature; but native religions contain no such hubris. Native traditions see human beings as simply a part of nature, and experience the trees, rocks, rivers, and animals as kindred rather than subjects or, heaven forbid, natural resources.

The ceremonies of native peoples are profoundly rooted in the earth. Many of them begin with an invocation of the four directions, establishing their rites within a sacred circle of goodness, health, and belonging. The seasons are likewise sacred, as the wheel of the year grounds daily life in a pattern that is not linear but cyclic. Everything in nature is holy, everything is in its place to promote life and balance, and humans are only truly healthy when they, too, walk with awe and respect for the whole.

Huston Smith, in his amazing book, *The World's Religions*, tells of a Native American Onondaga prayer he witnessed that lasted nearly a full hour. During that time, none of the people present closed their eyes, and everyone listened to the prayer in their native tongue. Smith understood nothing, but when he asked what had been said, was told the entire prayer was devoted to naming everything in sight, animate and inanimate, including spirits of the place, inviting all to join in the proceedings and to bless them.

The Onondaga were not conducting their service as dominators of nature, but as part of it, respectfully inviting all aspects to participate. The Navajo bring the entire world into their homes, as each dwelling is seen as participating in and representing the whole of the cosmos. For native peoples, all things in nature, including humans, have their rightful place, which must be honored; all things are kindred, brothers and sisters, and worthy of respect. They invite us to think not of humans embedded in nature, but of nature seeking to extend itself, growing into new forms and more complex patterns; to behold itself, developing humans as organs of self-awareness.

Later traditions, both Eastern and Western, saw nature as something that needed to be beaten back with a stick, and viewed salvation as a way to escape it. This has resulted in attitudes that have had disastrous effects on our environment, because we do not honor the earth as a sacred presence, but as a thing to be plundered and used at will.

But native traditions know better. They know that we humans are inseparable from the natural world, and in these traditions salvation is seen as the encouragement of natural cycles. Since the disruption of natural cycles threatens the tribe, these cycles of fertility, of growth and harvest, must be participated in and encouraged for the survival of all things.

This is a powerful form of mysticism, where no distinction is made between natural and supernatural, and where there is no divorce of human society from the ecosystem that supports it. There is only the body of the earth, often portrayed as the great goddess, of whom we are all a part, from whose womb we are born, and to whom we will return, to live again in some other form, as the cycle of life succeeds from one season to another, one generation to another, one era to another.

To know oneself as part of this larger self is to *truly* know oneself. One can participate in this mystery by encouraging and cooperating with the cycles of nature—by bearing children and making art, by giving due attention to the cycles and seasons of the earth, acknowledging and honoring the personified forces of nature—the gods—by performing the sacred rituals and telling the sacred stories.

Nature Religion Today

As Judaism, Christianity, and Islam spread throughout the Western world, the gods of the common people were subdued even as their people were conquered. The word "pagan" comes from the Latin *paganus*, which means, very simply, country folk, or common people. And indeed, as we know from the history of Europe, the church had quite a time ferreting out those who held to the "old ways" and continued to worship the old gods.

Indeed, it was never completely successful in this—although it tried. Christian society carried on an amazingly successful "smear" campaign against pagan believers. They called them witches, and by some counts, the church burned nearly nine million women in the Middle Ages for the terrible crime of honoring one's family traditions, for the knowledge of what herb can cure a specific ailment, or for believing that certain amulets or incantations might attract love or repel the evil eye. In fact, most of those burned were not witches at all, yet it is a terrible crime nonetheless, even if they all had been believers in the old gods. It is religious genocide, a holocaust largely ignored today, one of the most profoundly shameful events in the history of the Christian church.

Indeed, many people today are fed up with the ideological tyranny of the Abrahamic religions, the violence against other peoples propagated in the name of the one God—and with the environmental violence that has resulted from the specious distinction between ourselves and the natural world, which the religions of the one God have inspired. Many are returning to the native religion of their own ethnic peoples. Those from the British islands are beginning to practice once again the old ways of the Celts, while many of African descent are rediscovering Yoruba and other native African religions.

And though many of those who practice the old ways refer to themselves as witches, more often people will refer to themselves as "Wiccans," from which the word "witch" derives. "Wicca" actually comes from the Old English word *wicce*, which means to shape or bend. Wiccans call on the power latent in the natural world; and through their prayers and rituals, they seek to "bend" that power for healing or for the common good. Wiccans cherish their mythology, and in retelling the stories of the old gods they find new interpretations that speak to their contemporary experience and provide guidance for their spiritual and moral lives.

Many in Western society still buy the medieval propaganda that witches are in league with the devil, but in fact, nothing is further from the truth. Satan is a spiritual being that belongs to the Christian hierarchy, and has no place in any pagan system. Witches do not worship Satan, because they do not believe in Satan. Satan is a Christian belief. It is difficult to accuse someone of worshipping a being that she or he does not believe in.

Modern-day neo-pagans are not out casting spells trying to cause trouble for people, either. There is a strong belief in the pagan community that any energy that you put out there by means of a spell will come back to you threefold. That is certainly a powerful reason to put out good energy and not bad!

Wicca has had a very important impact on our culture in recent years. It is one of the fastest growing religions in the United States and Europe, and it is not hard to see why. It has been extremely healing and empowering for women, who, perhaps for the first time, are being encouraged to take responsibility for their own spiritual lives instead of handing their spiritual power over to an all-male clergy. Even more healing, the Goddess allows women to see themselves reflected in divinity, something that the all-male single-parent family of the Trinity never did.

But it has been empowering for men also. Everyone in Wicca is a priest or priestess, and everyone is empowered to take their spirituality into his or her own hands and to fashion a thing of beauty out of it.

The Power of Story

Not only are the native traditions different from other world religions, they are about as different from one another as they can be. The tribal rites of Uganda look very little like the Celtic rituals, and both are very different indeed from modern, urban neo-pagan circles. What they have in common, however—besides the belief in many gods—is a religious intuition that myth is more important than doctrine. Native traditions do not have systematic theologies, as we have come to think of them. Instead, they have *stories*— stories of gods, demons, humans, and half-breed beings in between; stories of treasure and loss, of failure and redemption, of the underworld and the abode of the gods. A college professor of mine once said, "Myths are stories that make sense of our lives," and the myths of every culture have served exactly that purpose.

The ancient Greeks explained the changing of the seasons by telling the story of Persephone, who was dragged by Hades to the underworld, where she was made to stay for four months out of the year. Her mother, Demeter, furious at Hades for stealing her daughter, swore that while she was there, nothing would grow upon the earth, creating winter.[1]

The Yoruba people in Africa explained that some people are prettier than others—and even sometimes deformed—because the god who shaped human beings from clay was drunk when he did so.

These are not scientific explanations, of course, but people would not begin to think "scientifically" and call into question their myths until the Greek philosophers began the trend over 2,000 years ago. Before that, humankind had been content with the explanations their sacred stories provided for millions of years.

Though we want scientific explanations these days for genetics, for why the sun rises and sets, and other mysteries of nature, there are mysteries of the human soul that science cannot begin to explain. For these mysteries, stories are still the best tools we have to help us understand ourselves.

Though our modern economy is based on scarcity, and society is stratified into the haves and the have-nots, matters of the soul are not sufficiently valued for people to hoard spiritual resources. This is both sad and fortunate. Sad because a single soul is infinitely more valuable than a Ferrari, and fortunate because there is no scarcity of stories, the very food of the soul.

We are fed on stories from birth. Our parents read stories to us on their knees, we watched stories unfold during Saturday morning cartoons, we heard them every week in Temple or Sunday school, or in our other places of worship. We thrilled to them as children, we gravitated to other sorts of stories as teenagers, and if we were wise, we returned to the simple tales of our faith traditions as adults, with new ears.

We also make our own stories. The stuff of these stories is our lives, and we tell them to one another constantly. We relate our dreams to one another over breakfast, we gossip about co-workers at lunch, and we tell stories of our workday over dinner. At night we watch the stories of other people's ordinary—or not-so-ordinary—lives on television or at the cinema.

We tell these stories to each other for the very same reason our ancestors told stories of the gods and heroes around the campfire—we seek meaning in our lives. We relate our dreams to our spouse because we hope that together we might be able to tease out some meaning from the bizarre imagery. We gossip about the ditzy clerk three cubicles away at lunch—and don't look so high and mighty, you've done it, too—because it makes us feel better about ourselves to see someone else more inept than we. We talk about our workdays over dinner because we discern that somewhere in the mix of struggle, frustration, and achievement, our lives are valuable and worth the living. And then we collapse on the couch and observe the stories of others, not only because we want to expand our knowledge beyond our direct experience, but because on some real and mystical level, their stories are our stories.

In watching others live out their dramas at the movies or on television, or in listening to a friend relate a recent adventure, we extrapolate and learn things about ourselves. The ancient Gnostic Christians taught that humans are not born with a soul, we have to make it during our lives if we are to have anything left once the body falls away. We must nurture our soul and feed it. We feed it with stories, both in the telling, and in the hearing.

Spiritual guidance sessions provide safe space for sharing these sacred stories—stories of our own lives, the lives of our loved ones, as well as a place to ruminate on the myths we have inherited, the myriad stories about the gods we hold dear. Talking with a spiritual guide helps us to reflect on these stories and to discern their meaning for us with intention. In the presence of a compassionate and supportive friend—or friends—the guidance room becomes sacred space. This is now the circle where the exploits of gods and humans are told, where meaning is found, where our souls can be nourished to grow, and where the Heart of Heaven becomes manifest to us.

Many Stories, Many Methods

Myths in native traditions are anything but monolithic. Stories shape-shift and replicate in the telling, and most cultures have multiple creation myths, many of them contradictory. Even the Bible contains two conflicting creation accounts in the opening chapters of Genesis. No matter. Each myth has something of value to relate, or it would not have survived. People do not tell stories that do not serve a purpose. And just as there is no one right myth to explain any one phenomenon, just as there is no one right story that provides meaning for all of us, just so there is no one right forum for the telling of these stories.

Mentoring. As spiritual guidance has evolved over the centuries, many forums for storytelling emerged. Probably the oldest is the mentoring relationship. Mentorship happens informally all the time, and has probably happened this same way since we began walking upright and carrying sticks. We are just naturally attracted to people whom we perceive as wise, who possess some knowledge that we lack. And mentors, from time immemorial, have often viewed the transmission of their knowledge as a sacred duty.

In later ancient societies this role was formalized, as those who aspired to be, say, healers or blacksmiths apprenticed with those who had mastered these arts and then eventually started practices of their own or sometimes took over their masters' practices. In time, these new "masters" mentored students of their own, completing the cycle. Along with the trade to be learned, the apprentice would also, hopefully, pick up valuable life skills, ethical and moral principles, and sometimes even knowledge of how his or her trade contributed to the life of the spirit.

For those who were spiritual masters, it was little different. An experienced shaman often apprenticed an aspiring student, who eventually, after learning the sacred stories and rituals, became a shaman in his or her own right. Masters particularly well-known for their shamanic power, holiness, or skill as a teacher often attracted larger groups of students. Called gurus in the Hindu tradition, wise women in the native Celtic traditions, roshis in the Zen tradition, or rabbis in the Jewish tradition, this master-disciple relationship has stood the test of time and is still employed in many traditional societies.

If you are studying to be a spiritual guide today, you have probably known both sides of this relationship. Most of us have been mentored—either formally or informally—by those we considered to be a little farther down the spiritual path than we, and if we are of sufficient age, have probably known those who have sought guidance, instruction, or at least advice from us.

Finding a mentor is usually an organic process—it happens naturally, without being sought out. Nobody puts out a shingle advertising him- or herself as a mentor (and you should probably beware of anyone who does). Likewise, if you put yourself out there as a mentor for someone, be prepared to be rejected. Mentors and those they mentor usually find each other, and some magical serendipity happens that both parties recognize. It's a bit like falling in love—no one controls it, it just happens. The bond between mentor and mentoree is often unspoken; no formal arrangement is made, no money changes hands, no expectations are voiced.

But this does not mean that the relationship is unimportant, or that the mentor should not be intentional and responsible in fulfilling his or her role. It is a sacred relationship, and if one is going to be a mentor, one must be cognizant of the profound responsibility one has—for the mentor holds the soul of the other in his or her very hands.

Sometimes the person seeking guidance is sufficiently aware to ask for mentoring directly. This is ideal, as the mentor can then discuss the parameters of the relationship, and also communicate clearly what will be expected of the aspirant. This formalizes the relationship, and one must be careful when mentoring to allow the seeker to do this. If it remains informal, the best thing to do is simply enjoy it, and impart what knowledge one can as responsibly as possible.

In your ministry as spiritual guides you will have opportunity to be a mentor to many people, in both formal and informal ways, in both professional and personal environments, in long-term relationships and brief encounters.

Mentoring is part of the abundance of the economy of grace that is the world. Mentors are provided for you precisely when you need them, and likewise people will look to you to mentor them at the proper time. It is both a privilege and a responsibility, and just as you have received, so should you give in return. Spiritual gifts do no good if they are hoarded—they are to be shared, and freely.

Epistolary Guidance. Mentoring, and its formal counterpart, apprenticeship, is as old as human relationship, but once human beings discovered writing, a new form of sharing our sacred stories was made possible. Buddhist scholars wrote the words of the Buddha down into sutras so that people in distant places could also benefit from the master's teaching. The Jewish prophets wrote their warnings down so that they could be read in distant cities to call the people back to a right relationship with one another and with their God. In the Christian tradition this method goes back as far as St. Paul's famous letters to the fledgling communities in Rome, Corinth, and other cities in Asia minor.

"Epistolary guidance" is a fancy way of saying spiritual mentoring by writing letters back and forth. As you can imagine, this became quite a popular method, as the scriptures of the major world's religions attest. If all the epistolary spiritual guidance that has ever been written were to be gathered into one place, there is surely not a library on earth that could contain it.

Though most of these letters and writings have been lost, it is to our great benefit that so many have survived. From the *Letter of Baruch* to the correspondence between Abelard and Heloise, these writings bear witness to more than merely history—they continue to bear fruit for those who read them today with a willing and inquisitive spirit.

Epistolary spiritual guidance is not simply an artifact of history, however. It continues to be a very popular form of spiritual guidance, especially since the advent of e-mail. Like mentoring, epistolary spiritual guidance can be a formal or an informal arrangement. Informal epistolary guidance is most common today, but this method is experiencing a rebirth as a formal practice.

I myself have had three e-mail clients, and can attest from personal experience that it can be just as engaging and fulfilling as other forms of spiritual guidance. It is not for everybody, of course—no one form of spiritual guidance is—but for those who enjoy writing, and who benefit from long periods between letters to ruminate over their replies, it can be a very effective form indeed.

One-on-One. In the fourth century of the common era, a new method of spiritual guidance emerged. It began when those who had been part of the persecuted and underground Christian Church saw their beloved community twisted beyond recognition by a horror they never expected: acceptance. When Christianity became the favored religion in the Roman Empire, the quiet and pious home-based rituals morphed into extravagant public rites that bore little resemblance to what had gone before. Horrified, these long-time believers fled to the desert to try to recapture the sincerity and austerity of the faith they held so dear.

The desert fathers and mothers were not necessarily ordained clergy, or people of any particular social standing. Most of them were probably even illiterate. They had no credentials or certificates to recommend them. Most of them were simple souls seeking their own peace and spiritual succor in the wilderness, and at first their encounters were probably informal ones with other monks and nuns.

Eventually, however, many of them gained reputations for being particularly wise in spiritual matters. Before long, other monks and nuns heard of their fame by word of mouth, and traveled long distances to seek them out. People from the cities also heard of their wisdom, and were not far behind. Perhaps several times a year, a householder or housewife would make the journey to one of the desert fathers or desert mothers, and in the quiet of the guide's cave, this person would tell his or her sacred story. The desert father or mother would listen, and if it seemed appropriate, might give some advice to the seeker. But the telling of stories and listening to those stories comprised the lion's share of what happened in those holy meetings, and the same is true today.

It is a sad fact that for most of the Christian tradition, this ministry was subsumed into the sacrament of confession, claimed as the purview of the ordained clergy, and often used not for the telling of sacred stories, but for the enforcement of dogma. But this was never the whole story, for there have always—even in the Christian tradition—been women directors, and nonordained male guides as well, though these were often relegated to monastic life or the fringes of the tradition.

St. Ignatius in the sixteenth century did a great deal to popularize formal spiritual guidance among the laity in his own day, but it is only now, in the last thirty years, that we have seen the formal ministry of one-on-one spiritual guidance explode. No longer the purview of ordained Catholic men, over time we have seen Catholic women, then Protestant men and women, then Jewish rabbis and laypeople, then Buddhists, Wiccans, and even agnostics take up this ministry as their own. The ministry of one-on-one spiritual guidance is part of the spiritual heritage of every people. We are indebted to the Catholic tradition for its formal structure, but just as the adventures of an endless variety of gods and goddesses were told around the campfires of old, there is a corresponding diversity of sacred stories being told in the offices of one-on-one spiritual guides today.

Each of these guides has his or her own personal style, but in a typical spiritual guidance session, one might expect to be invited to be seated, to get comfortable, and to find one's center. A candle might be lit to symbolize the presence of the Divine, and then the telling of stories may begin. The spiritual guide will be interested in many stories, but it is the sacred stories, those that tell of one's relationship with the Divine that will be of the most interest, and it is not unusual for the spiritual guide to refocus the conversation when the stories go too far afield.

Above all, it is the responsibility of the spiritual guide to provide a clean, safe, and comfortable space for the telling of these stories. Spiritual guidance, then, is primarily a ministry of hospitality: a spiritual guide provides a hospitable space for awareness of one's soul to emerge and notices when it does. He or she guards the space against environmental distractions and intrusions, and internal diversions and resistances.

As this ministry has developed in recent times, it is almost always intentional. The spiritual seeker and guide usually covenant together, either verbally or in writing, about what will be expected from each party. How long will the sessions be? How frequently will the client and guide meet? Will there be financial compensation for the guide's time; if so, how much? What will happen in the case of a missed appointment or an emergency? What if there is a spiritual emergency on the part of the client and he or she needs to speak to the guide before the next scheduled appointment? These and other questions are usually negotiated early in the guidance relationship, and doing so can prevent much misunderstanding and disappointment.

The one-on-one model has become normative for intentional spiritual guidance, and is usually the form assumed in the rest of this book. Insights from this model are of course applicable to almost any of the other models. There is no one right model, and an active spiritual guide will probably employ most of them at some point in the course of his or her career.

Group Spiritual Guidance. Though one-on-one spiritual direction is by far the norm, group spiritual guidance is gaining popularity. A group usually consists of a small number—usually between four and ten people. They will often sit comfortably, in a circle. They may begin with a centering exercise, or simply a few minutes of silence. Often the group will proceed with a brief "check-in," where everyone in the circle has an opportunity to say how they are, and what kind of a space they are in that day or evening. They may even share about how something that came up from the group's last meeting has affected their lives in the interim. After all have had a chance to weigh in, a theme for group exploration may be introduced, and the real work of telling stories can begin.

Often a group will form around an issue that requires discernment. A synagogue may have lost its focus or momentum, and members may be reevaluating who they are and what their mission is. Or a group may form around healing from religious abuse, or around women's approaches to spirituality. The reasons for starting a group are endless, but the benefits are many.

In one group I participated in, the Festival of the Holy Names, members formed around the issue of whether or not they could call themselves Christians. Each of us had experienced significant wounding from our traditions of origin. During the course of our meetings (which lasted over two years) we confronted such questions as: What does it mean to follow Jesus? What is the church? What does evangelism mean? As a way of addressing issues of power in Christianity, we took the Roman Catholic Mass and broke it into sections. We took each section and asked each other, "What was this originally intended to convey? Why doesn't it mean that for us anymore? How can we make it relevant again?" In this way we rewrote the entire Mass, and began performing it without any regard for who was clergy and who was not. By the end of our time together, we had each experienced significant healing, and felt freer to participate in our religious communities. The work of the group being done, we moved on to a different focus and format.

In more traditional groups, participants are screened and selected before the first group meeting, and members are asked to commit to being present at every meeting. There is usually a leader who moderates the meetings, leads meditations, and facilitates the particulars.[2]

Another very effective format is the Wisdom Circle. In a Wisdom Circle, decisions are made by consensus, and leadership within a group may rotate as people feel ready. Wisdom Circles also may be more relaxed in what they ask from members in terms of commitment. Wisdom Circles may take a "drop-in" approach, open to anyone who shows up. Boundaries in such groups are much more fluid; as members may show or not, the group is open to new people and—if the group is open-ended as far as how long it will meet—may be open to refocusing and redefinition as the members of the group change, both in terms of personalities and personal needs.[3]

Twelve-step meetings are probably the most popular form of group spiritual guidance, though most members are probably unaware that they are functioning as part of a larger tradition. Twelve-step meetings have their own traditions and a very specific focus, usually achieving abstinence from alcohol, nicotine, or other substances. Other twelve-step groups meet around issues of social timidity, controlling emotion (or not being controlled by emotions), living with addicts, or any number of other recovery issues. Most twelve-step meetings incorporate one-on-one mentorship into their practice, in the form of the twelve-step sponsor.

While most spiritual guidance groups meet in person, experiments have been made—and quite successfully—holding such meetings in chat rooms online. No doubt we shall see more of this sort of experimentation in the future.

Brief Spiritual Guidance. While we normally think of spiritual guidance as being an intentional, long-term activity, the truth is that the vast majority of guidance happens through accidental, one-time meetings between individuals. Perhaps you are a chaplain, and you know you are only going to see a patient once or twice. Perhaps you meet someone on the street who is facing a life-changing dilemma, or dealing with some kind of trouble. Just listening to a stranger's story may make an enormous difference to her or him. You may find that you have this, and only this, opportunity to say a word of wisdom, to model a healthy behavior, or lend a helping hand that may change the trajectory of a person's life forever.

In such situations, a spiritual guide may be able to help a person focus on the presence of the Divine in the ordinary, rather than dwelling on transcendent experiences (or the lack of them). If a person is fixated on the past, it may help to ask him or her what the Divine may be saying to them in the present. You may be able to suggest a spiritual practice, deconstruct a bit of "stinkin' thinkin'," help someone get something off his chest, or lead someone in a guided meditation to help her redirect her attention or energy.

Duane Bidwell, in his excellent article, "Brief Encounters,"[4] also reminds us that the majority of people who come for spiritual guidance only come for one or two sessions. Beginning spiritual guides are often dismayed when this happens to them, and are likely to ask "What did I do wrong?" Usually, the answer is that the beginning guide did everything right. Frequently, people simply do not come back. Perhaps what came up in the last session was too scary and they were not ready to face it, perhaps intentional spiritual guidance does not work for a certain person, or perhaps there is no chemistry between the guide and the client. Beginning directors should remember that this is normal, and should not take it personally.

Retreat Facilitation. Some spiritual guides, once they have received their training, take jobs at retreat facilities, or may begin offering retreats themselves. There is a long tradition in spiritual guidance in both the East and the West of offering retreats, and it remains very popular around the world. In some Buddhist countries, it is normal for adolescents to go into the monastery for a couple of years to receive spiritual instruction. People frequently will go for retreats featuring intensive meditation practices that may last from a few days to a few months. Though people usually meditate in groups, individual guidance sessions with a Zen master or a guru are often part of the retreat experience.

In the Western Christian tradition, St. Ignatius pioneered a series of "Spiritual Exercises" on which many retreats are based, even today. These exercises are a combination of guided imagery and personal reflection. The retreat leader vividly describes a series of scenes from the life of Jesus, with a "you are there" immediacy so that participants have the experience of actually being present. Participants later process what came up for them in these meditations in private spiritual guidance sessions. Thus, the Spiritual

Exercises provide a retreat experience that combines group participation and one-on-one guidance.

Retreats are a marvelous tool for people looking to deepen their spiritual lives. Often, retreats meet around a theme or a stated goal, such as "Finding Your Inner Authority," "Praying through Watercolor," "Justice Making," or a host of other possibilities. Retreat facilitation can be extremely rewarding for both leaders and participants, and may also be one of the more lucrative activities for spiritual guides in private practice.

Institutional Coaching. Finally, we are seeing a new ministry—institutional coaching—emerge from the business world. Sometimes a spiritual guide is called to help a sangha, a church, or a nonprofit organization discern its call to the community, or help it through a difficult transition. To do this, a guide might contract with a group for a certain number of meetings. At these meetings, the spiritual guide may provide a safe and sacred environment for everybody's stories to be told and heard. After listening closely to the stories, the guide may offer his or her "noticings" and may offer suggestions for how the group may achieve its goals, or how to bring its practices and its stated ideals into harmony. Some are taking ministry to the corporate world, offering spiritual guidance groups to employees. Others are offering "spirituality at work" groups that function very much like the Wisdom Circles mentioned above. Others may be doing ethical or depth discernment for employees, or offering staff retreats for corporations. Some guides are helping CEOs learn to be good stewards to their personnel, even teaching them spiritual guidance skills to act as a supervisor, so that the CEO can facilitate discernment for employees.

Spiritual guides can help institutions discern their spirit and their responsibility to the community, or integrate a sense of transcendent meaning into their corporate vision. Whatever the stated purpose, most spiritual guides working in a corporate environment help those they minister to move toward healthy ways of being, identify dysfunctional patterns, and provide interventions when needed.

Institutional coaching is a ministry in its infancy, but its potential is enormous as corporations are waking up to the importance of ethical and spiritual health in the work environment. Trained spiritual guides are rare in the corporate world, and it is a niche that will no doubt see exponential growth.

Just as the native traditions provide for us an endless assortment of sacred stories that continue to speak to our lives today, so there is unfolding before us an equally endless variety of venues in which these sacred stories—including the sacred stories of our own lives—can be told and held with respect and compassion, and where meaning may be sought and made. The simple model of the circle of storytellers around the campfire has given way to a kaleidoscope of methods, yet the function has remained the same: to enter into sacred conversation, tell our stories, evoke the Divine, and draw near to the Heart of Heaven.

Just as our tour through the development of native traditions was far from comprehensive, just so the varieties of spiritual guidance we have briefly mentioned is far from complete. Each of us has a personal style, and though the majority of us will practice at least one of the models discussed, many of us will also forge new models out of creative necessity and the needs of those we companion. In the next chapter we will begin to learn some essential skills to help us be effective spiritual guides, regardless of what model we choose to employ.

2

Taoism and Nondirection

It was with great frustration that Lao-Tzu packed his yak. He had tried and tried to instill in his disciples a sense of the great Tao. He taught them that if they could live with attention to the flow of the universe, their lives would be easy. But they were clueless. Nobody seemed interested in the great Tao, and he tired of trying to explain what was essentially ineffable. Finally, he gave up on his students. In fact, he gave up on humanity altogether as a lost cause. With a heavy heart he tied the last bundle to his yak, and headed for the wilderness where things were sane.

Just before his wisdom was lost to us altogether, he came to the top of a mountain pass, the last outpost of civilization. The gatekeeper there had heard of Lao-Tzu's teaching, and he pleaded with Lao-Tzu to commit his philosophy to paper before he left humankind forever. Dubious as to whether that would do any good at all, the old man agreed. The resulting book, consisting of just over 5,000 Chinese characters, became the famous *Tao Te Ching*, which means "the book of the Way and its power."

In our last chapter we discussed native traditions, in which humans do not see themselves as separate from nature. Taoism is one of China's native traditions, and it views humanity and nature as being similarly inseparable. We human beings are simply a part of nature. The Taoist sees him- or herself as equal to all other things in creation, and in fact, it is from observing nature that wisdom is gleaned. There is no revelation in Taoism. There are no gods. Nature reveals everything we need to know, if only we have the eyes—and the patience—to see it. Nature, in Taoism, is always correct and has the answers to every problem. Humans think too much and that gets us into trouble.

Taoism is not a fixed or solid tradition. There are many versions of Taoism; for instance, there is popular Taoism as practiced today, which is a highly developed shamanistic religion like many native religions. There is also what Huston Smith calls Esoteric Taoism, which merged with Buddhism over a thousand years ago and evolved into the Ch'an school of Buddhism, known in Japan as Zen. Esoteric Taoism no longer exists as a living, practiced religion separate from Zen or Ch'an. What we are left with, then, is Philosophical Taoism, which is as close as we are likely to get to "original Taoism." It is with this that we are primarily concerned here.

Taoism does not rest on a particular set of scriptures that it considers inspired, but more on a way of looking at the universe suggested by the ancient mystics in their writings. The most important of these are *Chuang-Tzu*, *Lieh-Tzu*, and, of course, the *Tao Te Ching*.

So what is this Tao thing Lao-Tzu talks about? This is a difficult question, and Lao-Tzu tells us right off in his first poem in the *Tao Te Ching* that "the Tao that can be described in words is not the true Tao." Like most mystics, however, he does not let the impossibility of his task deter him, and spends the next eighty poems trying to do just that. Many of us are used to thinking of deity in terms of God or the gods, but Taoism demands a very different orientation. The Tao is not a god, ruling over subjects, or wielding power over nature—the Tao is a part of nature, or more accurately, nature is a part of the Tao, and therefore the Tao is not a separate personality, like the Jewish or Christian God. The Tao is simply that which is. By observing nature we can discern certain characteristics about it, and also discern healthier ways of being human. There is no one to pray to in Taoism, there are no rites to be performed, no liturgy to be recited. There is simply the world as it is, and we will either find our proper place within it or we will suffer.

According to Lao-Tzu, all things in nature are in balance. The Tao consists of both yin and yang, opposing forces that define and sustain each other: action and rest, light and dark, matter and spirit. The *Tao Te Ching* speaks of matter and spirit as if they were partners, one incapable of functioning without the other. Taoists speak of spirit as "nonbeing," implying something that exists in objective reality, but which possesses no physical manifestation, or "being." Synonyms for spirit/nonbeing are emptiness and nonexistence. This unitive vision of spirituality is difficult for Westerners reared with pervasive dualism. Lao-Tzu asks, as if speaking directly to us, "Being both body and spirit, can you embrace unity and not be fragmented?" (poem 10).[5]

To illustrate his vision, Lao-Tzu presents nonbeing as absolutely necessary for physical realities to "function," and vice versa, saying, "Thirty spokes join together at one hub, but it is the hole in the center that makes it operable. Clay is molded into a pot, but it is the emptiness inside that makes it useful. Doors and windows are cut to make a room, but it is the empty spaces that we use" (poem 11).

The first time I read these verses, chills ran down my spine. I felt that I had been told a great secret that was the most obvious thing in the world: in the relationship between matter and spirit, one is not dominant. "Existence and nonexistence produce one another." Lao-Tzu explains, "Existence is what we have, but nonexistence is what we use."

The Philosophy of Freedom

Lao-Tzu's most famous disciple was Chuang-Tzu, who lived in the third century B.C.E., in a district of China known as Meng, which most scholars locate as being near modern-day Honan, south of the Yellow River. We know a great deal more about Chuang-Tzu than we do about his master. His first name was Chou, and he worked for a while in the state lacquer garden. But due to his disregard for propriety and rules, it is not likely that he held the job for long. This was probably just fine with Chuang-Tzu, who was deeply influenced by the Taoist philosophy of Lao-Tzu, and took his master's teachings about "not doing" to heart.

Much like Plato writing about Socrates, Chuang-Tzu's writings recount many tales of Lao-Tzu, and expand upon his philosophy. Just as Socrates wrote nothing and Lao-Tzu wrote little, both Plato and Chuang-Tzu wrote voluminously about the teachings of their mentors, complete with their own unique spin, of course.

Chuang-Tzu was surrounded on every side by zealous moralists dictating the proper way to do just about every aspect of a person's life. These were the Confucianists, who followed the philosophy of Confucius, naturally.

Confucius began with an egalitarian message: noble birth does not convey nobility. A person is as noble as he or she behaves, and everyone can strive to be a superior person. But being a superior person was a lot of work: there was a proper way to do just about everything. Confucius piled on the rules until even a person who had all the money and leisure in the world could not be properly observant. It was into this world, obsessed with Confucian rules and regulations, that Chuang-Tzu was born.

In Chuang-Tzu's philosophy, one did not need to memorize the Confucian rules for being a superior person, nor did one need to keep them. The endless harangue of how one *should* be, or what one *should not* do irritated him, and seemed to him not only pointless, but destructive. And this is why: according to Chuang-Tzu, everything is okay exactly as it is. The universe is One, Chuang-Tzu taught. The moment you say something is not okay, you make a distinction and do violence to the whole. Once you start making distinctions, once you say something is good, it implies that something else is bad—and suddenly you have up and down, hot and cold, pleasant and unpleasant, right and wrong, good and evil, useful and useless, light and dark, big and little, ad infinitum, ad nauseam. All of these things are illusions created by the human mind. The 10,000 things rise from the One and fall back into it again. Seeing the One instead of the 10,000 things is not hard to do, and is the only way, in Chuang-Tzu's system, to stay sane.

"Life, death, preservations, loss, failure, success, poverty, riches, worthiness, unworthiness, slander, fame, hunger, thirst, cold, heat," he writes, "these are the alternations of the world. . . . Day and night they change place before us and wisdom cannot spy out their source. Therefore, they should not be enough to destroy your harmony."[6]

The efforts of Confucius and the other moralists were pointless, he said. Human nature is human nature, it is what it is, it is part of the Tao. Trying to change it is crazy, and doomed to failure. "The Way has never known any boundaries," Chuang-Tzu tells us, "So, those who divide fail to divide; those who discriminate fail to discriminate. What does this mean, you ask? The sage embraces things. Ordinary men discriminate among them and parade their discriminations before others. So I say, those who discriminate fail to see."

Not surprisingly, Chuang-Tzu is an iconoclast. Skewering sacred cows is one of his favorite pastimes; he delighted in bursting the bubbles of every self-inflated ideologue who crossed his path. One of his best friends,

Hui-Tzu, was also his constant foil. One time Hui-Tzu said to him, "I have a big tree in my yard—it has a trunk that is so gnarled and bumpy that it is absolutely useless to any carpenter. Your teaching is just like that tree—big and useless!"

"And yet," Chuang-Tzu said, "it had the wisdom to grow so gnarled and bumpy that no axe will ever touch it. Nothing will harm it. If there's no use for it, how can it come to grief or pain? And is it really useless? Why don't you relax by its side and do nothing? Or lie down underneath it for a free and easy nap?"

Unlike Confucius, who spent most of his adult life chasing after political appointment, Chuang-Tzu eschewed all political power. One story relates that Chuang-Tzu was fishing in the P'u River when the king of Ch'u sent two officials to him to offer him the job of governor. Chuang-Tzu just continued fishing and without even turning his head, said, "I have heard that there is a sacred tortoise in Ch'u that has been dead for three-thousand years. The king keeps it wrapped in cloth and boxed, and stores it in the ancestral temple. Now, would this tortoise rather be dead and have its bones left behind and venerated? Or would it rather be alive and dragging its tail in the mud?"

"It would rather be alive and dragging its tail in the mud," said the two officials.

Chuang-Tzu waved his fishing pole at them and shouted, "So go away, and leave me to drag my tail in the mud!"[7]

Chuang-Tzu knew that the moment he accepted such a post, he would cease to be a free man. Suddenly there would descend upon him responsibilities and stress, and expectations and propriety, and all the things that steal a person's freedom. And that is the secret to understanding Chuang-Tzu. His philosophy can be reduced to one word: freedom. Freedom from all the things society tells us we *should* do or *should not* do, freedom from stress and striving, freedom from arbitrary rules that senselessly shackle us.

And it isn't just freedom from the expectations of society. Chuang-Tzu finds the lives of those who eschew the world and go off to live in caves to be just as imprisoning. There's nothing free about the ascetic ideal with its fasting and silences and self-conscious denial of every earthly pleasure. Instead, Chuang-Tzu's philosophy advocates freedom from the ideologies, prejudices, rules, structures, proprieties, and all the anxiety that comes in the wake of all such man-made nonsense.

Chuang-Tzu teaches that all loyalties are suspect, including one's loyalty to the state, to one's ruler, to one's family, to an ideology, or a religious doctrine. The only loyalty that has any value is the loyalty to one's true nature, to the Tao itself. Instead of chasing after cockeyed notions of "right" and "wrong" Chuang-Tzu invites us to see beyond such arbitrary distinctions and to rediscover an authentic way of being in the world. He wants us to respond with authenticity, rather than through the filters of propriety; to react humanely—as a human would—to any given situation, just as a fish reacts as a fish would, or a bird reacts the way a bird would.

Not bound by artificial rules or rituals or scripts, human beings, Chuang-Tzu says, can discover who they are truly meant to be. "*Be*" is the operative word, not what they are to *do*, what they are to accomplish, what they can achieve—but who they are to be, in their most unaffected, unmediated, and authentic selves. Only by discovering this true self can one hope to, in Chuang-Tzu's words, "stay in one piece, keep oneself alive, look after one's parents, and live out one's years."

Chuang-Tzu tells us, "You never find happiness until you stop looking for it." Happiness can be found, but not by striving. "The pursuit of happiness" enshrined in the Declaration of Independence would have seemed backward to Chuang-Tzu. One is happy only when one ceases pursuing and striving and *trying*, and allows oneself simply to be.

The Way of Nondirection

Chuang-Tzu tells the story in his book of a boatman guiding his boat across a river. If another boat, an empty boat, is adrift on the river and appears as if it might collide with the boatman's own vessel, he is not likely to get very angry, even if normally the man is a very bad-tempered person. He will calmly push the other boat away and continue on his voyage. If, on the other hand, there is someone else in the other boat, the boatman will most likely scream at him and shake his fist in the air. Why is this, Chuang-Tzu asks? All because there is someone in the other boat. So, if you can empty your own boat, no one will oppose you, and your life will be easy.

The practice of spiritual guidance rests on very few skills. The most important of them all is the ability to empty your own boat. To be an effective guide you must remove a lot of things from your boat before you ever sit with a client. You must remove the notion that you know what the spiritual life looks like and how to live it—your spiritual path and your client's spiritual path are two very different things and may bear absolutely no resemblance to one another. You must empty your boat of any agenda—you do not know from session to session where the Divine may be leading your client, and if you have a plan it will only interfere and obstruct the process. You must remove from your boat all of the anxieties and worries you normally carry with you—you cannot be fully present with your client if you are thinking about what you are going to fix for supper tonight. You must also empty from your boat an expectation that you have to perform—you are not the spiritual guide, the Divine is the spiritual guide. You are simply there to bear witness to what happens and to point out what you notice along the way. In other words, you don't need to worry about whether you are doing it right, because there is nothing to do—which brings us to another important Taoist principle, *wu-wei.*

Wu-wei literally means "not doing," and it is the most important skill you will need to learn as a spiritual guide. Westerners have a very difficult time with this concept. It seems like laziness, and yet, for us who have been conditioned to go-go-go, just stopping and being is very hard to do. Lao-Tzu writes, "When Heaven gives and takes away, can you be content to just let things come or go? And even when you understand all things, can you simply allow yourself to be?" (poem 10).

He also promises, "Who can wait for the storm to stop, to find peace in the calm that follows? The person who is able to wait patiently in this peace will eventually know what is right" (poem 15).

Slowing down enough to hear the voice of the Spirit, or to observe the Way of the Tao, is, in my experience, one of the most important spiritual disciplines of all, and the primary skill in the ministry of spiritual guidance. An old joke reminds us that Westerners say, "Don't just sit there, do something!" while Eastern wisdom says, "Don't just do something, sit there!" The value of not doing is every bit as great as the value of nonbeing, or spirit, and our effectiveness as spiritual guides rests entirely on our ability to *not do.*

This has not always been seen to be the case in the history of spiritual guidance in the West. In the past, religious systems were much more proscriptive and directive in their approach to guidance. A young Jewish man who met with his rabbi for spiritual guidance a hundred years ago would probably receive more instruction than listening. Likewise, in the

Christian tradition, where most spiritual guidance was given in the confessional, the priest may have started out by listening to a person's sins, he (and of course it was always a *he*) would spend the balance of the time admonishing, instructing the person, and, of course, assigning penance. The Eastern traditions have been little different, as gurus and roshis are famous for their own admonitions and lectures.

Yet, in the last fifty years or so, another method has arisen, informed by the evolving practice of psychotherapy, where listening has replaced instruction. This "nondirective" method is now the normative model in most spiritual guidance training programs around the world, and is considered superior by most to the old, directive model, as it jettisons the arrogance so tightly clung to in the past by spiritual guides, and actually provides room for the Divine to lead the seeker in novel ways that may be more appropriate to the individual. The day of cookie-cutter spiritual formation is over, and guides are now better instructed in what *not* to do than they are in what *to* do. Taoism speaks to this nondirective approach exquisitely, and in addition to not doing, Lao-Tzu and his progeny likewise instruct us in not forcing, not trying, not being attached, not being arrogant, not being judgmental, not acting like someone we are not, and not taking things too seriously. In the rest of this chapter, we will explore these nondirectives, informed by Taoism's rich wisdom.

Not Forcing

The *Tao Te Ching* concerns itself greatly with leadership, both political and spiritual. Not surprisingly, Lao-Tzu astounds us with a parable about the power of water:

> In the whole world nothing is softer than water.
> Even those who succeed when attacking the hard
> and the strong cannot overcome it
> because nothing can harm it.
> The weak overcomes the strong.
> The soft conquers the hard.
> No one in the world can deny this
> yet no one seems to know how to put it into practice (poem 78).

The ability to be strong in the way that water is strong is a mystery that Lao-Tzu says no one can quite grasp, and yet it is nevertheless the only way to be truly successful. Even though no one "knows how" to do it, truly spiritual people seem to evidence this power without trying: "The sagely person is like water," Lao-Tzu says. "Water benefits all things and does not compete with them. It gathers in unpopular places. In this it is like the Tao" (poem 8).

Learning to be like water involves the practice of *wu-wei*. Unlike just learning "not doing" as we discussed above, *wu-wei* calls us to a deeper understanding that might be called "not forcing."

The Taoist watches nature and sees that what nature does—eroding mountains, growing forests, making rivers—is accomplished effortlessly. Being one with the Tao, nature goes its own way and forces nothing; and yet grand works and great beauty result. *Wu-wei*, therefore, isn't inactive at all, but is activity at its most efficient, because it accomplishes without effort. When the sage, recognizing oneness with the Tao, acts upon his or her environment in the spirit of the Tao, then, as Thomas Merton writes, "His [or her] action is not a violent manipulation of exterior reality, an 'attack' on the outside world, bending it to his conquering will: on the contrary, he respects external reality by yielding to it . . . a perfect accomplishment of what is demanded by the precise situation."[8]

When it comes to the issue of leadership, especially spiritual leadership and spiritual guidance, Lao-Tzu asks us pointedly, "Loving all people and leading them well, can you do this without imposing your will?" This is a great and important question for us, who are surrounded by traditions notorious for spiritual coercion. Unfortunately, we often unwittingly perpetuate the cycle of coercion. It is easy for us to think that the answers we have found after our own many years of search and struggle are the "right" answers for everybody. But Taoism suggests that, like water, all things simply flow out and return, void of any notions of "right" or "wrong."

Not Trying

The key to being successful in spiritual leadership, according to Lao-Tzu, is to not try. "Therefore the sage, not trying, cannot fail," says Lao-Tzu. "Not clutching, she cannot lose." Likewise in our own spiritual lives, "the truly good person does not try to be good." Goodness needs to come naturally, effortlessly, like breathing or hearing. The sage is not concerned with being good, or even with being a good spiritual guide. He or she does not give it a thought. It is not a goal. The goal is to respond humanely—as a human would—to whatever situation life gives.

This advice is congruent with the attitudes of other spiritual guides I know, but I have rarely heard these principles expressed as clearly or evocatively as Lao-Tzu does. Most spiritual directors would not dream of "forcing" their clients into a practice before they are ready, nor would most initiate violent interventions into the lives of their clients. But it is sometimes difficult to articulate why we believe this.

A gift of the *Tao Te Ching* is giving us not only words to describe our experiences, but illuminating what we already know. Lao-Tzu might be speaking specifically about a spiritual guide when he writes, "The sage who leads says: 'I practice "not doing" and the people transform themselves. I enjoy peace and the people correct themselves. I stay out of their business affairs and the people prosper. I have no desires and the people, all by themselves, become simple and honest.'"

Nonattachment

Lao-Tzu also advocates good spiritual guidance technique by suggesting that we let clients make their own discoveries. Instead of telling them what they need to know, it is far more effective for seekers themselves to make the associations and experience the epiphanies. As Lao-Tzu says, "The best leader puts great value in words and says little, so that when his work is finished the people all say, 'We did it ourselves!'"

It is best for us not to put too much stock in programmatic systems of spiritual growth or formation, since in pursuing the effectiveness they offer, they can sometimes blind us to what is going on for clients in the here and now. Lao-Tzu warns: "When you organize, you must of necessity use names and order. But given that, you must also know where to leave off naming and structuring. Knowing when to stop, you can avoid danger" (poem 32).

It is difficult for us to simply let go of the end result, to not strive or push a client, especially if we are impatient with his or her progress. We may have somehow come to believe that processes such as enlightenment or conversion are instantaneous occurrences. In reality, however, this is almost never the case. Spiritual maturity is a slow, difficult process; the seeds that were planted years ago slowly take root, and even more slowly blossom. Much of the time we may not even be aware of just when growth is occurring because in a sense it is happening underground like the developing seed. As spiritual guides, we need to trust that the Divine constantly whispers to all people, and needs little help from us.

We would do well to relinquish our attachment to the outcome of a single session or even the duration of a seeker's involvement with us. This is hard because, as we sit with people, hear their struggles, and get to know their foibles, we begin to love them. We care so much for the people we minister to that we are often unaware of the ways we attach ourselves to their "progress" and growth.

Lao-Tzu counsels that we should give of ourselves to others without any hope of success or fear of failure: "The sage makes good on his half of the deal and demands nothing of others." The sage is not concerned with getting anything back because with the Tao all things flow out and return.

This is not to say that we should not care about people; rather we should not be attached to immediate results. To care, to love, to invest ourselves in others is part of what makes us human and holy. Lao-Tzu says, "The sage's heart is not set in stone. She is as sensitive to the people's feelings as to her own. She says, 'To people who are good, I am good. And to people who are not good? I am good to them, too.' This is true goodness. 'People who are trustworthy, I trust. And people who are not trustworthy, I also trust.' This is real trust" (poem 49). If we can learn this kind of trust in the nature of things, I believe we can be more effective listeners and companions.

Not Arrogant

Perhaps the most important truth Lao-Tzu has to teach spiritual leaders is humility. Potential clients come to us because we are "people in the know," who they often believe are "spiritually advanced" and able to help them begin the journey.

The truth, which most if not all spiritual directors know well, is that we are all beginners; much of what we have come to know simply reveals how little we actually do know. Lao-Tzu tells us, "Those who know, do not speak. Those who speak, do not know" (poem 56). Those concerned about guiding others with integrity find that spiritual maturity simply increases our awareness of our shared humanity and leads to a more compassionate rapport with the seeker. As the Christian mystic Mechtild of Magdeburg says, we should live "welcoming to all," expecting to learn as much from our clients as we hope they may learn from us.[9]

The goal for any spiritual guide is to maintain a genuine and vital relationship with the Divine and the universe, and then to attend to others' spiritual lives. Lao-Tzu tells us that "One who is well grounded will not be uprooted. One who has a firm embrace will not let go."

Both grounding and embracing are essential. Grounded in our tradition, we will not be led astray by passing whims of spiritual fancy; embracing the traditions of others, we inherit vast wisdom. My spiritual experience as a Christian need not be divorced from my study of Taoism. Cultivating relationships with the wisdom of other traditions informs and enriches our practice in so many ways: by adding to our repertoire of divine images, by enlarging our understanding of how others experience the divine presence, and by augmenting our worldview with other models and potentialities. Nothing external impacts us as greatly as taking in the wisdom of others—be it a client's observations or the great Lao-Tzu's—and allowing those seeds to germinate deep in the soil of our own spiritual garden.

Not Recognizing Distinctions

Similar to Lao-Tzu's instruction not to be arrogant by assuming we know it all, is Chuang-Tzu's instruction to eschew distinctions. In the mysticism of Taoism, all things are one, and distinctions are illusions that blind us to the ultimate unity of all things.

In his book, Chuang-Tzu tells us the story of Lao-Tzu's funeral. One of Lao-Tzu's disciples, Ch'in Shih went to the ceremony to mourn for him. There was a long and complicated ceremony planned, observing all the proper Confucian rules for proper mourning. But Ch'in Shih simply stepped into the room, uttered three loud cries, and left. Outside, another disciple caught up with him. "Weren't you a disciple of the master?" he asked, enraged.

"Yes," Ch'in Shih replied.

"And you think it's all right to mourn this way?"

"Yes," said Ch'in Shih. "Lao-Tzu happened to come because it was his time to do so, and he happened to leave because that is the way things happen. If you are content with the time you have and are willing to let things happen the way they happen, then grief and joy have no hold on you. In the old days this was called being free from the fetters of God. When the firewood has been burned up, the fire just goes somewhere else."

Just as Ch'in Shih eschewed notions of how his teacher "ought" to be mourned, so we should give up our own notions of how spiritual guidance "ought" to be done. Each of us is a unique manifestation of the One, and our ways of providing spiritual guidance will be equally unique, equally suited to who we are, rather than who we think we "should" be. There is no one "right" way to mourn, nor is there one "right" way to provide spiritual guidance.

To be an effective interfaith spiritual guide, we must also jettison the idea that there is one "right" religion to practice, one "correct" god to worship, one "orthodox" teacher or teaching, or even one "proper" way to live a human life. In fact, Chuang-Tzu would counsel us to throw any notions of "right" or "wrong" out the window. Spiritual guidance is most effective when it is done without regard to teachers, systems, religions, methods, or models. Instead, we sit together and simply concentrate on being ourselves. I am most effective when I can sit with a client and simply be "John the human," not "John the Catholic," or "John the Jungian," or even "John the nondirective spiritual guide." If I can simply respond as a human would, without regard to tradition or teaching or any other distinction with which we categorize and label our lives, then I can be truly present, and my heart will be as open as the sky.

Not Taking Things Too Seriously

When Chuang-Tzu himself was about to die, his disciples started planning a sumptuous funeral for him. Not surprisingly, he protested, saying, "Why do you need to do anything? I will have heaven and earth for my coffin and coffin lid, the sun and moon for the pennies on my eyes, the stars and constellations for my jewelry, and the ten thousand things for my parting gifts. The furnishings for my funeral are already prepared—what more is there to do?"

"But if we don't bury you," his disciples protested, "the crows and kites will have at you!"

Chuang-Tzu calmly replied, "Above ground, I will feed the crows and kites; below the ground I'll feed the crickets and ants. Tell me, what do you have against the birds?"

Most of us feel that death is no laughing matter, and yet Chuang-Tzu approached even this taboo subject with great humor. It is easy for us as spiritual guides, especially when we are just starting out, to be deadly serious about our work. This is not surprising—we want to do a good job, after all, and we want to avoid doing anything that might wound our clients or impede their growth. Yet, it is possible that in taking ourselves and our work too seriously, we may end up inflicting the very distress we are hoping to avoid. We must remember that it is not we who are doing the work. It is the responsibility of the Divine to weave the web of being. We are there to hold the space and bear witness. And if we can do that with a bit of good humor, so much the better. For we do not see ourselves clearly if we take ourselves— or our clients—too seriously. Humans are often ridiculous beings. Silliness is a part of being human, and will manifest itself any time we are being authentic. We will do violence if we hold any distinction too firmly, even the conviction that what we do has some kind of ultimate value. What happens in the direction session is not the be-all and end-all in a client's spiritual life. It is likely that nothing you say or do will make or break your clients' spiritual evolution. Not taking ourselves or our ministry too seriously is an antidote for the kind of arrogance we discussed above.

Not doing, not forcing, not trying, not being attached, not being arrogant, not being judgmental, not acting like someone we are not, and not taking things too seriously, these are the primary techniques needed to be an effective spiritual guide. Lao-Tzu promised that those who cultivate these things "will have true goodness. Cultivate these in your community, and goodness will catch on. Cultivate these in the World, and goodness will fill the Universe."

3

Hinduism and the Many Faces of Divinity

In the Upanishads there is the story of a father trying to teach his son something about the nature of Divinity and the world. He told his son to put a handful of salt into a bucket of water. The boy did so, and soon after went to bed. After breakfast the next day, the father told the little boy, "Bring me the salt I gave you last night."

The little boy looked and looked, but he could not find the salt anywhere in the bucket of water. The salt had dissolved. "I can't find it, father," he said, distressed.

"How does the water at the top of the bucket taste?" his father asked him.

"It's salty!" the boy's eyes lit up.

"Pour a little off, and tell me how the water in the middle of the bucket tastes."

The boy did so, and tasted it. "It's salty, too!" he reported.

"How does it taste at the very bottom of the bucket?" asked his father.

The boy poured off some more water and tasted it again. "Even saltier!" he said, making a face. The father told the boy to toss the rest of the water out and to come and sit on his lap. When the boy wriggled up, he told his father, "I think the salt will always be in that water, now."

His father nodded, and said, "Remember how you were asking about God, and why could you not see him?" The boy nodded. "The world is a bucket of water, and God is the salt. You cannot see it, but it flavors everything. This is the truth, my son. You are salty, too."

This is the sublime truth of Hinduism: Divinity permeates all things, including us. For those who know how to see, there is no part of the universe that is not brimming with Divinity. In fact, for Hindus, there is nothing in the universe that is not both Divine, and at the same time also *us*. The Sanskrit words the father used in our story above are, "Tat Tvam Asi," which mean, "You are that." This applies to everything, from the highest godhead to the lowest dung heap. Everything is us, and everything is Divine.

That is because Hinduism, much like Taoism, teaches that the separations between things, the distinctions, are illusory. The fact that there appear to be distinct beings and things is a charade. None of it is real, none of it has any ultimate value, other than simply this: the entertainment of the deity. According to the Hindu faith, the universe is *lila*, a Sanskrit word that means, "play." The world is God's playground, a vast illusion spun solely for the amusement of the Supreme Being. All that we see is fabricated, a show, and all of our struggles, our suffering, our joy, our drama, and our happiness exists solely for the enjoyment of the observer.

And we, too, are just illusions. We seem to have personalities, we appear to ourselves to have independent consciousness, but this, too, is an illusion. In Hinduism there is only one thing in the universe: God. And all the myriad beings that populate this world are merely bits of God at differing stages of awareness of their true identity. The world, then, is an enormous game of peekaboo that the Divine is playing with itself.

This is no secret in the Hindu faith, and the tradition is filled with myths and rituals that try to bring this truth home to us. For once one has pierced the veil of seeming separateness, and realized that everything in the universe—including the Divine—is identical with oneself; then the spell, the illusion, is broken, and one can enjoy—and know that one is enjoying—true union with the Divine. Illusion no longer has any hold over a person, and the endless cycle of reincarnation is broken.

Seeing everything and everyone as Divine is a fine mystical idea, but it is not always easy to do. In our work as spiritual guides, however, it will be our primary activity, and Hinduism has much to teach us about looking for—and noticing—the Divine in unlikely places.

The Development of Hindu Mysticism

Hinduism's mystical teaching did not fall from heaven, fully formed, of course. It took a long time for it to develop into the subtle and complex mystical system that it is today. When Hinduism began, it was simply a nature religion like others we've been studying. The gods were personifications of natural forces: Indra, the god of thunder and king of the gods; Agni, the god of fire; Vayu, the god of wind; and literally thousands of other local nature deities are attested to in early Hindu literature.

The most famous early Hindu scripture is a collection of hymns called the Vedas. No one knows when they were written, but it is a good guess that they go back as far as 5,000 years or more. The Vedas are largely composed of hymns to Indra and the other early Hindu deities, and revisions of the Vedas were compiled to arrange these hymns for liturgical use. There was no talk of play among the gods in these early myths—in fact, the business of the gods was deadly serious. In one myth we are told that the gods did not start off as the gods at all, but as demons opposed to the gods. The gods and demons worked together to churn the ocean into soma, the magical elixir that granted unlimited life and power to any who drank it. Then, when the gods weren't looking, the demons stole the soma and drank it. They, then, became the new gods, and the old gods became the demons.

The terms "gods" and "demons" don't necessarily refer to the morality of the beings involved, but to their power. Those with the power are the gods, those without the power became, by default, the demons, the enemies of the gods. Religious practice at this time was concerned with the generation of *tapas*, the Sanskrit word for "heat," which also means "spiritual power." Demons could become holy men, and by means of sacrifice, gain enough *tapas* to be a threat to the gods. Likewise, the gods need the sacrifices of human beings, but they don't want humans to be *too* holy, or their *tapas* would rival their own, and also pose a threat to their supremacy. The gods in Vedic Hinduism, then, are concerned with maintaining a balance of power: keeping the gods fed with sacrifices, but also keeping humans and demons in their places.

Sacrifice was the primary means of worship in Vedic Hinduism, especially the fire sacrifice. As the priestly caste grew in influence and wealth, the sacrifices gradually became more and more elaborate and difficult to perform, not to mention expensive. At the height of the Vedic period, the horse sacrifice often took weeks to perform, involved the killing of hundreds of horses, and nearly a score of priests working around the clock to do it correctly. One slip, and it would have to be started all over! (The last known horse sacrifice was performed in 1986, and filmed for posterity. And just to relieve your squeamishness, gourds were sacrificed in place of actual horses.)

About this time a major shift occurred in Hinduism. Nobody knows how it happened, but someone discovered that the sacrifice could be performed internally rather than externally. By the use of vivid imaginal practice, a person could perform an entire sacrificial ritual in his head. Not only was this far cheaper than killing hundreds of horses, but it seemed to be just as efficacious as the physical ritual.

Suddenly there were all of these priests sitting still, going through this long, fourteen-day ritual in their heads. What do you think is going to happen? One of them veers off into the bliss of meditation, and *boom*! enlightenment. One of them, and then another of them, had the experience of unitive consciousness as a result of their imagination experiments, and suddenly meditation was born.

These holy men realized they were on to something, but it was not a popular discovery among the priestly caste, for a number of reasons. First of all, anyone can meditate and know this sublime mystery, which threatened their monopoly on spiritual power in their culture. Anyone could become a yogi. Second of all, the experience of unitive consciousness had grave implications for their theology, in effect, invalidating it. The mystery they glimpsed in meditation went far beyond the placation of nature spirits upon which the entire edifice of Vedic Hinduism was built.

The Upanishadic Shift

Though the priests tried, however, they could not stem the tide of this new religious awareness. People of other castes began meditating and they too, had the same experience of unitive consciousness, and Hinduism quickly transformed into a very different animal altogether. It went through what I call the "Upanishadic shift," named after the new scriptures that were appearing to explain and document this new awareness, the Upanishads.

According to the Upanishads, there is only one being in the universe, which these writers call Brahman. Brahman is the ultimate ground of all things, yet inside each and every being is a corresponding spirit, the Atman. The Atman is that bit of Brahman that lives in each of us. Brahman and Atman are one being: you and the Divine are one being.

Thus it came to be seen that all of the Vedic gods were merely parts of Brahman, the one being who fills the universe. But Brahman did not have much of a personality, apparently, because Hindus quickly supplanted him with gods they liked better, especially Shiva and Vishnu. Ultimately, in Hinduism, it doesn't matter what you call this one being: Brahma, Shiva, Vishnu, Kali, Durga, any name will do. For though there is only one being, that being can wear any face. One has merely to discover the mask of the Divine to which one feels the most attraction, and pray to that face. I have read that there are more Hindu gods on record than there are living Hindus! In Hinduism, it doesn't matter which god you appeal to: they are all the same god, in the end.

There is a wonderful myth that illustrates this Upanishadic shift.[10] Indra, the king of the gods was building a gigantic palace that would be a fit reflection of his glory. But every time he visited the royal carpenter to see how the work was progressing, he got another idea of how to make it larger, grander, more worthy of his greatness. Finally, the carpenter got completely stressed out, and realized that if Indra kept making more and more demands, he'd never be done with the project. So he went to Brahma, the creator, and explained his problem. Brahma was sitting on a lotus that grows out of the navel of the sleeping Vishnu. Brahma told the carpenter to go home, something would be done to help him.

The next day a beautiful blue boy, surrounded by other children, appeared at the gates of Indra's palace. Indra summoned the boy to him, and said, "So why have you come to see me?"

"I have heard that you are building a marvelous palace, more grand than any Indra before you has ever built."

"What do you mean, 'Indras before me'? I am the only Indra there is!"

But the boy laughed at him and said, "That's what you think. I have watched Indras come and go, come and go. Vishnu sleeps in the ocean of the cosmos, and the lotus that grows from his navel is the universe. Brahma sits on the lotus, and when he opens his eyes, a world comes into being, and that world is ruled over by an Indra. And when he closes his eyes, the world disappears, and its Indra disappears with it. Each Brahma lives nearly

500,000 years. Then the lotus dries up, and another grows in its place. How many Indras have there been? How many drops of water do you think there are in the ocean?"

Just then, Indra noticed an army of ants marching across his palace floor. The boy pointed at the ants and said, "See those—those aren't ants at all, they're all the Indras that have ever been."

Needless to say, Indra, who thought he was the highest god in heaven and earth, was brought down a notch or two, as were the Brahmins, the professional clergy. This story certainly illustrates the shift that happened in the popular religious imagination, as Hinduism morphed from a polytheistic nature mysticism to a qualified monotheism, becoming one of the most complex and satisfying mystical systems the human race has ever known.

The Hindu Trinity

Hinduism reveres every god in its past, but reserves the pride of place for Brahma, the creator; Vishnu, the sustainer; and Shiva, the destroyer. These three are sometimes known as the "Trimurti," or the Hindu Trinity. Brahma isn't really worshipped all that much, but he does get a lot of lip service. Most Hindus today honor either Vishnu or Shiva as the most supreme expression of Divinity, and just as Catholics and Protestants have fought wars over which system is right, so Vishnites and Shivites have fought each other over which god best represents the supreme reality.

Shiva is a scary fellow, and full of contradictions. He lives in a graveyard, and dances on the bones of the dead. He is an ascetic, and master of the practices advocated by the yogis, especially meditation. But he is also a husband and father, and together with his consort, Shakti, he is the master of the Tantric schools of mysticism as well. In Tantra, the man assumes the identity of Shiva, the woman assumes the identity of Shakti, and in their sexual union the illusion of separateness in the universe is dissolved, creating a fast track to enlightenment that is not only expedient, but a heck of a lot more fun than sitting your butt down in the ashes of the dead muttering mantras all day.

Vishnu, on the other hand, is not nearly as scary or weird. Vishnu is the preserver of life, and constantly intercedes on earth to make sure that the balance of power is not upset. "Whenever evil seeks to destroy the sacred order," Vishnu says, "I take myself a body and put things right." Vishnu has had many incarnations, being born into a human body to be the savior of humankind, over and over again. Krishna is probably the most famous incarnation of Vishnu, and Rama is a close second. Vishnu incarnates in much the same way as Jesus is understood by Christians to be the incarnation of Yahweh, the Jewish God. (In fact, since Hinduism can honor any god as a face of the one God, ever since its contact with Christianity, Jesus has been, in fact, seen by Hindus as an incarnation of Vishnu.)

Vishnu does not ask his followers for heroic ascetic practices, as Shiva does, but instead offers a much more devotional path. One can reach liberation from the cycle of death and rebirth by the grace of Vishnu, merely by worshipping him. We might call it the lazy man's path to enlightenment, but that would be inaccurate, especially if you have ever been to one of the marathon mantra sessions the Vishnites love so much, where they can go on for *days* chanting the names of Vishnu. It may be the path of love, but it's still a lot of work.

But this is part of the genius of Hinduism: there is no *one* right way to reach liberation. The path that is right for me may not be the path that is right for you. Hinduism recognizes four broad paths: the way of knowledge, the way of devotion, the way of compassionate action, and the way of psychophysical exercises.[11] Any of these paths can bring you to unitive consciousness. And it makes sense: if there is only one thing in the universe, the Divine, then any path you take is going to lead you back to the Divine in the end. You just have to find out which path is *your* path, and walk it, just as you have to decide which face of God is the right one for *you* to worship.

Hinduism is a mass of contradictions and competing impulses that is both compassionate and dispassionate. It has room for both the pacifist and the warrior. It is moral and amoral, simple and complex. In fact, just as it is almost impossible to say what Hinduism *is*, it is equally difficult to say what it is *not*. It has subsumed into itself every religious tradition that has come into contact with it, and all without any system of centralized authority. Its magic is derived from that one very simple mystical insight: "*Tat Tvam Asi.*" No matter what you look at in the universe, your mother, your cat, the sky, a hamburger, a fence post, or a pile of dog-doo on the sidewalk, the same mantra applies: *you are that.* Because there is only one thing in the universe, one being, and you are that being. We are all trapped in an illusory existence until we really, truly, at the core of our being, understand that truth.

Images of Divinity

Though the mystical awareness of Hinduism is easy to grasp cognitively, it is much more difficult to bring these insights to bear upon our daily life. The illusion of separateness—of me vs. you, us vs. them—is strong, and requires no small amount of practice to overcome. Fostering such awareness is a primary goal of the spiritual life for Hindus; and reminding people that the Divine is present in every part of life, indeed, in everyone we meet, is a large part of the work of spiritual guidance. Hinduism has much to teach us who are learning to guide others in their mystical awareness.

When Mel came to me for spiritual direction, she was quite distraught. Her spiritual path seemed to be taking her into some uncharted waters, and yet she was terrified that God would punish her for the new paths she was exploring, for the dangerous ideas she was thinking. A friend of hers had introduced her to Transcendental Meditation, and it had been a lifesaving practice for her. Sitting meditation was one thing, but what really scared her was that many of the mystical teachings of TM's native Hindu tradition made sense to her. She was raised a strict Wesleyan Holiness Christian, and she was terrified of going to Hell if she continued going the way she was.

It was clear to me that her meditation practice was life-giving to her, and that she was spiritually hungry for the teachings she was receiving. I asked her if she loved God. "Of course!" she snapped, and then she started crying. I asked her to describe her God to me. After a while her sniffles decreased, and she described a deity who demanded absolute allegiance, absolute assent to a long list of dogmas, and who would throw anyone who did not comply into a Hell of eternal torture without a moment's hesitation.

"Is this the same God you worshipped as a child?" She nodded, yes. "He doesn't seem to have changed much," I noted.

"God never changes," she parroted, something she had no doubt heard a million times at church.

"I beg to differ," I offered cheerfully. "You speak as if there is only one God. Yet, everyone sees God through the lens of her or his own experience. There are as many gods as there are people! And as you grow and change, the god of your experience grows and changes, too. It doesn't sound to me as if you have made room for God to develop much. You have grown and changed, but I think you are still hanging onto the god you worshipped when you were in third grade."

All of us have internalized images of the Divine. Some of them might have been helpful at some point in our development, others were destructive and painful. None of them should be mistaken for the truth. As Kant pointed out hundreds of years ago, we only experience the world through our own subjective lenses. There might be an objective reality out there somewhere, but we cannot know it. Just so, there might be a definitive image of Divinity out there somewhere, but human beings will never know it, because our experience and environment inevitably color every image we have.

When a seeker finds his or her relationship to Divinity painful, it is often important to ask him or her to describe the deity they are in relationship with. Very often the images they have internalized are limited, inadequate, or even destructive. Asking a client to articulate exactly what sort of being his or her god is will often provide a good place to start your work together.

As Mel and I sat together, she came to the painful realization that it was hard to love a being she was so afraid of. The god of her experience was distant and mean. She "loved" "him" because she was commanded to, but when she got honest with herself, she realized that she didn't love him at all. She feared and hated him.

"If you will pardon my saying so," I offered one day, "he doesn't sound like a god who is really worthy of your worship." This stopped her cold, and I noticed she was shaking.

"What choice do I have?" she asked.

We were almost at the end of our session, and so I asked her if she would mind doing a bit of writing between now and our next session. She agreed, and I asked her to describe the kind of god she most wanted to be true. "I'd like you to create an entirely fictional deity. Let your imagination run wild. What kind of god does your heart most desperately desire? I'd like to hear all about this god next time."

She returned with three pages of closely scribbled notes, and she wept as she read them aloud. "Wouldn't it be wonderful if this could be your god?" I said. She nodded.

"I have a suggestion. Why don't you fire your old god, and hire this one?" She looked at me like I had just informed her she had eaten a frog. "I can't do that!"

"Maybe not," I said. "But will you seriously consider it?"

The fundamentalist Christianity Mel had grown up with taught her that the Divine was a jealous being, and that it was dangerous to think outside of the box, religiously. Yet Hinduism is eminently sensible when it comes to one's image of the Divine. Hinduism provides an endless list of possible gods, and it does not matter which one you choose, since they are all just faces of the one God who has no attributes. There is wisdom here for us who have found ourselves saddled with destructive or even evil images of the Divine.

Just as the notion of individual people or gods or things is illusory in Hinduism, just so our notions of who "God" is, what "he" acts like, and what "he" requires are equally illusory. There are millions of possible gods to choose from; some of them are healthy for us, and some of them are not. Spiritual guidance is concerned with sorting out the positive from the negative images, and helping seekers to embrace those images that are helpful, and letting go of those images which are not.

This is some of the scariest work many of our clients will ever do, but it is also the most important. For until seekers find a concept of Divinity that will allow them to be who they are, to think the thoughts that are occurring to them, and can support them as they change and grow, then any attempts at spiritual progress will be frustrated, if not utterly impossible.

Tyrants and monsters do not serve humans well as deities. Submission to such gods inevitably results in unhealthy self-images and neurotic spiritualities that do not support people in the unfolding of their true selves. And passing on such images of Divinity to succeeding generations only compounds the difficulties. Although it may be scary at times, challenging such destructive images is the responsibility of spiritual guides. Giving clients permission to discard unhealthy images and to embrace healthy images is a common feature of our ministry, though the process may very well prove too frightening for some. They may not return. If this happens to you, don't feel bad. You may have planted a seed that will take years to bear fruit. The truth always brings freedom, even though it may take some time to do its work.

The Art of Noticing

Images of Divinity are often concerned with gods who are "out there" somewhere, in heaven, on the mountains, or just plain "elsewhere." Divinity may indeed be "out there" but that is only part of the picture. Hinduism teaches us that Divinity is ubiquitous—everything is "salty" as the father told his son in the story that begins this chapter. Divinity permeates the whole of the created order, including us. The Jewish scriptures ask, "Where can I go from your spirit? Or where can I flee from your presence? If I ascend to Heaven, you are there; if I make my bed in Hell, you are there" (Psalm 139). Likewise the Hindu mystical poet Nammalvar sees himself as drowning in Divinity when he writes, "I don't understand why, while all the worlds live within him and he lives within them by birthright, our lord . . . of gardens blowing with fragrance, should assault and devour this poor little soul of mine with his grace."[12]

Just as the father says to his son, "You are that," the Hindu tradition uses a related couplet to apply to Divinity: "You [God] are that; and you are not that." Divinity is in all things, but there is no thing that exhausts or defines Divinity.

A seeker's spiritual life is not defined by how well he or she follows rules or performs certain duties, but by the quality of relationship with the Divine. Relationship doesn't happen between a seeker and some absentee landlord, but between a seeker and the events, people, and attitudes that make up everyday living. In other words, if Divinity is not in the ordinary exchanges and events of one's daily living, Divinity is no more than a rumor.

A large part of walking with a client is helping him or her to notice the movement of the Divine in every aspect of his or her daily life. What is the Divine doing in his or her marriage? In his or her work? In his or her relationship with parents or children? What is the Divine doing in his or her spiritual community or social communities? What is the Divine doing in the political arena or in the larger scope of public life? Too often a seeker is simply too close to his or her own life to see clearly what the Divine is up to. This is where the spiritual guide excels, in the *art of noticing*.

When Sy came to Bridget for spiritual guidance, his reason for coming was that his prayer life seemed dry and uneventful. He went to synagogue weekly, but the prayers did not move him the way they used to. He was frustrated and depressed. "My wife doesn't understand," he complained. "She never had those feelings in synagogue in the first place, and I think it's hard for her to relate." As the sessions progressed, the fact that Sy's wife no longer went to synagogue with him emerged as a point of contention in their relationship—especially as they were expecting a child in a few months, and Sy was concerned that they worship together as a family.

As Bridget companioned Sy it was revealed that his wife gained a lot of personal meaning from her volunteer work with the Sierra Club. Sy was sympathetic to the cause, but had never joined her for a meeting. "Has it ever occurred to you," Bridget asked him one day, "that your wife goes to Sierra Club events to pray?" He gave her a blank look, and she continued. "I don't know Judaism very well," Bridget admitted, "but I have heard of a Kabbalistic doctrine known as *tikkun olam*, which I think means, 'remaking the world.' I could be wrong, but my guess is that your wife goes to these meetings because she meets God there." As we will see in a later chapter, *tikkun olam*, remaking the world, is a spiritual practice for many Jewish people, and can embrace many forms of activism—any activity, in fact, that makes the world a better place.

Sy had focused on worship as having a specific form; it did not occur to him that it might take other forms less familiar or traditional. Bridget might have been in error—Sy's wife may not have gone to Sierra Club meetings for any mystical motivation at all—but from Sy's reaction, Bridget knew she had noticed something significant.

Mapping the Divine Life

The Four Paths of Hinduism. There is no sphere of human endeavor that is not ultimately bound up in the life of the Divine. As we have already seen above, the Hindu tradition recognizes four broad paths of spiritual practice: the ways of devotion, of knowledge, of work, and psychophysical exercises. Sy's path was devotion, and his wife's was work, but both are valid spiritual disciplines, and both are a form of relationship with the Divine.

The Four Arenas. A very valuable tool described by Jim Keegan, SJ, in his article "To Bring All Things Together," helps spiritual guides map, and notice, the movement of the Divine in the lives of their clients. Keegan doesn't give it a name, but since, like the Hindu formulation, it groups the Divine life into four "arenas" I have named it thus for the sake of this book.[13] As Keegan describes it; first, there is the Individual Arena, which is concerned with the client's interior life. This takes into account his or her thoughts and feelings, ideas and fears. Second is the Interpersonal Arena, which is the area of relationships: family, friends, lovers, even strangers on the street. Third is the Structural Arena, which includes all of the many paradigms we fit into: our place in society, the hierarchy of our workplace, our role in spiritual communities, our place in our family. This arena is concerned with all the many structures—often invisible to us as they are imaginal structures to begin with—in which we function. The final arena, the Environmental Arena, is concerned with the ambient climate: culture, nature, and the large part of creation that continues on despite our involvement, but which nonetheless impacts us formidably.

Spiritual guides using the Four Arenas may ruminate on where the Divine may be moving in each of these different arenas. This is an especially helpful technique to employ when the noticings are few and far between. This is common sense: if we are not noticing the Divine where we are looking, look somewhere else. It may be that we have been focusing on the Individual and Interpersonal arenas, and have, for the time being, exhausted the insights to be gleaned. A guide familiar with the Four Arenas, however, may be aware of this and switch his or her focus to the Structural or Environmental arenas, finding a plethora of noticings that he or she had just moments ago been blind to.

Paracelsus's Entia. Paracelsus was a Renaissance alchemist and physician who viewed humanity as being composed of three parts: physical, emotional, and spiritual. After many years of mystical study, he developed a system that, he believed, could lead to the eradication of all disease—physical, mental, and spiritual.

Disease, he felt, was caused by disharmonies in what he called the five *entia*, or entities. These *entia* are spheres of human endeavor that, until Paracelsus, were not thought of as being related. First there is the *ens astrorum*, or the historical field, containing the history and culture of a specific geographical place. Attention to place, and to a people's culture, is of utmost importance for one's health. The second *entia* is the *ens veneni*, the healthiness of one's food. Long before organic gardeners began warning us that toxic substances used in growing our food could be dangerous to our health, Paracelsus was beating a similar drum. The third *entia* is the *ens naturale*, or the innate predisposition toward health or illness we are granted by our parents. In other words, Paracelsus took genetics into account in his schema. The fourth *entia* is the *ens spirituale*, or the field of social endeavor, as Paracelsus was convinced that the healthiness of our human interactions had a great effect on our health as well. Today, we might call this psychological health. The final *entia* is the *ens Dei*, or that all-encompassing field that is

God, for as Paracelsus tells us, our relationship to God is just as important to our well-being as any other aspect.

Loosely translated into modern terminology, then, Paracelsus believed that God and humankind were joined in a common goal, the perfection of the universe—similar to *tikkun olam*—which could only be brought about by attention to our healthy relationships with our past, the healthiness of the substances we put into our bodies, the genetic predisposition we have toward disease, our psychological well-being, and finally, a right relationship with God.

Though not well-known in conventional spiritual circles, Paracelsus's system is another "map" that may help us plot the movement of the Divine in a person's life.

A Salty Life

With attention, a spiritual guide can help a seeker notice the Divine in every part of that person's life, for surely there is no part of anyone's life where the Divine is not. And the Divine is always at work, even when at rest. As the salt permeated every drop of water in the bucket, just so the divine life permeates every aspect of ours. Our goal in becoming spiritual guides is to become sensitive to the movement of the Divine in the most unlikely places— especially those places that are not obvious to our clients. Often we have little more to do than to simply voice what we see; our clients may yawn or react with the force of visionary revelation. Either way, we should keep our eyes open. Salt is *everywhere.*

4

Buddhism and the
Compassionate Witness

One of the greatest mystical teachings in human history began with a broken heart—a heart rent by compassion for the suffering of others. It was a most unlikely event, as the broken heart belonged to a prince who lived in luxury and never wanted for anything he could possibly desire.

The prince was Siddhartha Gautama of the Sakyas, a small kingdom in India approximately 2,500 years ago. According to legend, before he was born, his father consulted an oracle, who told the king, "If he remains in the world, he will unify India, and become its greatest king. But if he forsakes the world, he will become the greatest saint, and redeem the world." His father was not too keen on this saint business, but he wanted the former option very much indeed. So he set out to protect Siddhartha from any influence that might cause him to take up the path of religion. The king built high walls for the palace, so the young prince could not see outside. He surrounded Siddhartha with only beauty and luxury.

Despite his best efforts to shield Siddhartha from the painful realities of the world, the young prince one day traveled from one palace to another and along the way saw three things he was not supposed to see—three things that cut him to the quick and stirred his soul. First he saw an old man leaning on a cane. The king had never allowed the prince to see anyone older than the king himself. The prince stopped in his tracks at the sight of the old man. Old age—the idea had never occurred to him before, and he shuddered. He was also moved by the old man's vulnerability. He wanted to leap from his chariot and help, but his attendants dissuaded him.

Next, however, he saw a woman racked with disease. We don't know what sort of sickness she had, but the young prince had never seen anyone who had anything worse than a cold. Perhaps she was a leper covered with sores. The prince's attendants had to restrain him from running to embrace the sick woman—who knew what she had, after all? Siddhartha felt sick himself, and wanted to understand the mystery he was encountering—how widespread was sickness and disease? What was its cause and its cure? His head swam and his heart ached as his journey continued.

Not long after this, the entourage had to halt, for there in the middle of the road was a corpse. Siddhartha had never seen a dead body before, and the sight of it horrified him. "Is this my end and the end of all people?" he asked. He jumped from his carriage and, despite the protestations of his attendants, he cradled the dead man's head and wept. He had observed three griefs, and his heart had received three great blows, the last of which broke it utterly, and the young prince felt helpless and awash with compassion.

Finally he was persuaded to continue his journey. But before he reached his destination he saw something else he had never seen before, something that gave him hope. He saw a monk begging for alms. The man wore simple, rough clothes. He was unconcerned with commerce or wealth. He was lord over no one and had no cattle and it looked as if he had no home. Most striking of all, however, he looked happy—more than happy, he looked content.

Suddenly, Siddhartha's idyllic life seemed superficial and empty. Having learned about the realities of old age, sickness, and death, he desperately wanted to find an answer—an escape from these conditions. He wanted to help his people and alleviate their suffering. He could no longer lounge in his palace eating figs and sweetmeats, for all pleasure in these things had left him. The monk had shown him that there was another way to live, and he desired that life more than anything else.

So it was that one evening, under cover of night, the prince left his wife, his son, his father, indeed his entire kingdom behind. He had a broken heart to heal, and he would not rest until he had found the key to stop the suffering of all creatures.

For years Siddhartha threw everything he had into being a Hindu holy man. He sat under a couple of gurus, and lived and practiced with a group of forest-dwelling monks. The teachings he heard emphasized asceticism, so he starved himself until he could see his spine through his stomach. He lived exposed to the elements, and practiced many extreme techniques such as holding his breath until passing out.

After several years of this, Siddhartha said to himself, "This is crazy. If I don't knock this off, I'm going to kill myself. And then what good will I have done? There has to be a better way." With that he renounced asceticism, realizing that his body was the only vehicle for enlightenment that he had and that he had to care for it properly if it was going to be of any service to him. His fellow forest dwellers did not take kindly to this "heresy" and banished him from their company.

Undeterred by their opinions and derision, he found a place in the forest by himself and continued his practice. One day, after intense study, he sat down beneath the Bodhi Tree, and he vowed that he would not get up again until he had achieved enlightenment. The legends say that Mara, the evil one, tempted him with desire in the form of a beautiful seductress, but Siddhartha was unmoved. Mara then attacked him with terrible forces of nature—hurricanes and flaming rocks—but all turned to a rain of flower petals before touching him.

Mara then challenged his right to do what he was doing. Who was he, after all? He was a prince, not a holy man. He did not belong here. Siddhartha did not answer with words. Instead, he simply touched the earth, and the earth responded, "I bear witness"; all of nature roared. Mara fled, and Siddhartha sank into deep meditation. He removed himself from the center of his universe, and allowed his consciousness to expand until it was at one with everything. He became the compassionate observer, feeling the pain of every being, feeling moved and yet remaining unmoved in his determination.

And then, suddenly, he was no longer Siddhartha. He was Buddha, the one who is awake. In a flash of unitive awareness he saw through the veil of seeming reality to the deeper reality of which we are a minute part. He saw all of existence in one glimpse. He saw everything *as it is*. In this flash of insight, called "satori," he transcended his separate self and realized that all of the universe was one, and that he, too, was that one. He saw—and knew—that his most authentic self was not Siddhartha at all, but existence itself. His identity transferred from Siddhartha's ego to the cosmos in all its multidimensional glory.

He saw in that moment the impermanence of all things, that all things arise, and then fall again, only to rise again in new forms. He saw that the past is a shadow and the future is a dream, and that to live in either is to live in a fantasy world, for there is only the *now*. He saw that it is this very grasping after the illusory that causes so much of our suffering, and that we will continue to suffer so long as we resist what *is*.

In that moment, he not only transcended his ego, but also the cultural paradigms that ordered Indian society. He realized that every creature suffers and is worthy of compassion, from highest to lowest. The caste system—an idea central to Hinduism, which dictates who should serve and who should be served—became meaningless to him, and he saw all people as equal. (Unfortunately, there were some exceptions to the Buddha's clear sight—he still regarded men as superior to women, though he would soften on this as his ministry progressed.)

He likewise saw all of the Hindu teachers' talk of gods and religion to be utterly unnecessary. "There may be gods," he taught, "and there may not be. It is not important and has no bearing on reaching enlightenment." The Buddha adopted an agnostic view on most metaphysical matters.

This did not please everyone, of course. One of his students complained, "Whether the world is eternal or not eternal, whether the world is finite or not, whether the soul is the same as the body, or whether the soul is one thing and the body another, whether a Buddha exists after death or does not exist after death—these things the Lord does not explain to me. And that he does not explain them to me does not please me, it does not suit me." The Buddha would just smile. Sometimes the Buddha could be downright infuriating.

Because he had no need for gods or religious rituals, the Buddha did not claim for himself any divine authority. He didn't want people to accept his teaching out of fear or coercion or any religious illusions. "Don't take my word for it," he told his listeners, "instead, try the practice out and see if it works. If it does, use it; if it doesn't, discard it."

Thus, what the Buddha founded was not so much a religion as a technology; a method of practice that can help the seeker reach his or her goal. What is the goal? For the Buddha it was the ceasing of suffering. The first of his four Noble Truths, one of the most basic Buddhist creeds, tells us that "life is suffering." This sounds pretty dour, but the next three truths give us hope: "Suffering has an identifiable cause"; "It is possible for suffering to end"; and finally, "There is a path that can be followed to end suffering."

So what is that path? The Buddha condensed his teaching into eight principles that, if followed, can lead to liberation:

1. Right understanding
2. Right thought
3. Right speech
4. Right action
5. Right livelihood
6. Right effort
7. Right mindfulness
8. Right concentration

What constitutes what is "right" in any of these formed the basis of much of the Buddha's teaching as he sought to mediate the unfathomable to the clueless. Like Lao-Tzu, the Buddha was often frustrated with his students, but he persevered. Some of the members of his old forest community became his first followers, and before long his ministry flourished. People came from far and wide to join his community. People of low caste found that in the Buddha's community they found respect and equality. Eventually even his wife and his mother became nuns, forsaking the palace even as young Siddhartha had done, and walking the path to liberation. Buddhism has countless stories of the Buddha's compassion as he traveled the length and breadth of India. He lived to be a ripe old age, in fact. Some believe he was in his eighties when he ate one final meal and slipped away into rest.

His followers mourned his death, but remained true to his teaching. They passed his teachings along orally until the first round of scriptures were set to paper hundreds of years later. Though they no doubt had accumulated much mythology by then, the basic story of the little prince with the broken heart still shines through.

Compassion for One's Self

Those who followed after the Buddha worked diligently to record his words, to honor his memory, and to follow in the way that he pioneered. As time went by, however, different people in different places and times developed different understandings of the Buddha and his mission.

Those followers who cling to the most primitive form of Buddhism—by which I mean the least changed, the closest to what the historical Buddha actually taught in this life—are the Theravadans. "Theravada" means "the way of the elders." For Theravadans, the Buddha was simply a man who discovered a way to be liberated from suffering and the endless cycle of reincarnation. For these Buddhists every one must have compassion on him- or herself first, and compassion for the rest of creation will follow. There is no savior in this system. If one wants to be liberated, one must work the system until one succeeds. This way is sometimes called "the little raft" since if a person wants to get to the other shore he or she must row the raft for him- or herself—there is only room for one person on the raft.

This example has much to teach us as spiritual guides. If we are to be a compassionate witness for others, we must first attend to our own spiritual lives with compassion.

In her marvelous article, "The Compassionate Observer,"[14] spiritual guidance instructor Jane Vennard invited her students to just such a practice of compassion. Many of them were nervous about being spiritual guides for others. She asked them to write a list of all the reasons they could *not* be spiritual guides. They wrote things like, "I'm not wise"; "I'm not holy"; "I'm too judgmental"; and similar objections. Then she asked them to make a list of all the reasons they *could* be spiritual guides. Their new lists included such responses as "I'm a good listener"; "I've had a lot of life experience"; "I am a person of prayer"; and other affirmations. When they were finished with their lists, she invited them into a guided meditation:

> Allow your compassionate heart to expand. . . . Now open your eyes and read all the reasons you cannot be a good spiritual director, read them with compassion. . . . Now read the list of all the reasons you *can* be a spiritual director, read them with compassion. . . . As you read, know that everything you wrote on the first list is true . . . and that everything you wrote on the second list is true. . . . You cannot do spiritual direction and you can do spiritual direction. . . . From this place of compassion gently hold the paradox . . . you are not ready and you are ready . . . you do not know enough and you know all you need to know.[15]

After the exercise, one student realized a profound truth, "If I truly believe I cannot do spiritual direction I might keep myself from offering what gifts I have to another. If I believe too strongly that I can do spiritual direction, I might become arrogant and get in the way of the movement of the spirit."[16]

Spiritual guides must walk many fine lines, and this one between insecurity and arrogance is an important one. To witness with compassion both our vulnerabilities and our strengths, without judging ourselves (or "making distinctions" as Chuang-Tzu would put it) is a skill we must cultivate to be effective spiritual guides.

The old saying "Charity starts at home" has some bearing, here. We must practice being compassionate to ourselves—and develop some alacrity at it—before turning our gaze toward another. We must "paddle our own raft" so to speak before attempting to carry others. If we cannot view ourselves with compassion, if we cannot hold our own darkness and light with love we will not be able to companion others without projecting our own judgments onto them.

In our practice of spiritual guidance, we have plenty of opportunities to practice compassion, and indeed, our hearts will be broken as well, if we are practicing correctly.

Compassion for Others

Many Buddhists felt that the demands of their religion were too great. In order to reach liberation, one must really work at it as a full-time job. This left most people resigned to countless lives of reincarnation and strife. The Mahayana school developed to meet this need. These Buddhists held that a secret teaching was handed down orally from the Buddha—a teaching not recorded in the scriptures. This teaching said that when the Buddha died, he refused to enter nirvana until all beings were liberated. He became what is called a "bodhisattva," one who has vowed not to enter into his own rest until all creatures could do so. "Mahayana" actually means "the big raft." In this system, the Buddha paddles the raft, and it is big enough for anyone who wants to get onboard. It is not by one's own efforts that one reaches nirvana in this system, but through the grace of the Buddha.

Many devout people have followed the Buddha's example and have also sworn themselves to eschew nirvana until all can enter. Anyone can become a bodhisattva, anyone that is, who is so moved by compassion that they are willing to sacrifice their own rest and reward. The bodhisattva gazes upon all beings with compassion, and gives his or her life in the service of all beings so that they may find spiritual fulfillment.

Becoming a spiritual guide carries something of this commitment. We, too, commit ourselves to the spiritual progress of the people who come to us. We, too, are charged to view them with compassion and bear witness to their journeys. This is a large part of what we do as spiritual guides: bearing witness with compassion.

When Mark came to Lucy for spiritual guidance he was really beating himself up over his addiction to nicotine. He had tried many times to stop smoking, and every time he had failed. He was raised as an evangelical Christian and believed at some level that it was a sin. A liberal Presbyterian now, he no longer felt that God was going to send him to Hell for smoking, but he still felt like a moral failure.

It was obvious that he had just smoked a cigarette before coming to the session—Lucy could smell it on his clothes. A tangle of feelings fought with each other inside Lucy. She practiced Buddhist insight meditation, and decided that it might help her to employ that practice now. She told Mark that she felt a number of responses and would like to take a couple of minutes of silence to sort them out. He agreed and they sat together contemplatively for a time.

Lucy closed her eyes and allowed the different thoughts and feelings to emerge. Her grandfather had died of lung cancer; and she knew what a painful and undignified end that could be. One voice in her head was screaming at Mark that he was an idiot; he should do anything in his power to stop smoking—if he died then he only got what he deserved. While these thoughts might be seen as judgmental, she did not see them as such. She simply listened to these voices with compassion, knowing that they arose out of her own painful experience, her own fear, and her own genuine love and concern for her client.

Other voices were in evidence, too. As a longtime member of Overeaters Anonymous, Lucy had struggled with her weight. She knew that the chemical reactions that caused the cravings for nicotine and her own weakness for white chocolate were different, but her own struggle with addiction moved her heart toward Mark and his dilemma. She saw in him not a moral failure but a person coping with illness.

With equanimity and patience, Lucy resisted the temptation to move into judgment, and simply bore witness to Mark's pain and her own myriad responses. She was able to maintain her role as the compassionate witness to his journey without becoming condescending or directive.

Another Witness

It occurred to Lucy at this point that she was perhaps not finished with her meditation, and that more thoughts might be bubbling to the surface. Acknowledging the thoughts that had already arisen, she cleared her mind again to see what else would come. It occurred to her that the universe also had a perspective on this situation. It held Mark and sustained him, it called forth from him responsible actions and moved him to his own compassionate responses. Whether Mark smoked or not might have bearing upon how long he might be present to be of service to his fellow creatures, but Lucy had no doubt that Mark was an active force for compassion in the present. He was a tireless volunteer at his parish's soup kitchen and tutored school children one afternoon a week. The universe was *grateful* for Mark, she realized, not disdainful of him.

It then occurred to her that the universe did not abhor using Mark as an agent of compassion in the world simply because he smoked. But Mark's own self-loathing might so preoccupy him that the energy he normally put toward helping others could get thwarted and wasted.

Lucy had only been meditating for about three minutes when she opened her eyes and cleared her throat. But before she could say anything, Mark told her that he had had an insight. "I think I'm more angry with myself for smoking than God is." She nodded and smiled, and bore witness with compassion to the journey of the awesome creature in her presence.

The Zen school of Buddhism teaches a radical notion: all beings are already enlightened—they simply don't know it yet. All creatures are held in love by the Divine, or as Zen Buddhists would say, all beings possess Buddha nature. Everything is okay exactly as it is. This is the perspective of another witness—the Divine, or the universe itself, as Buddhists would say. When Siddhartha sat down beneath the Bodhi Tree, a number of conflicting forces were at war within him—his own compassionate desire to liberate all beings, and the forceful protests of Mara, who told him any number of reasons why he could not succeed. And when Mara asked him by whose authority he was doing all this, the prince simply touched the earth, and the voice of the universe was heard: "I bear witness."

Zen Buddhism resulted from the synthesis of Indian Buddhism with the native Chinese Taoism, and there is much of Lao-Tzu's *wu-wei*, or "not doing" in this approach. By simply bearing witness to Mark's pain, and to her own conflicting voices, Lucy was able to faithfully hold intact the sacred container of the session as the Divine and Mark were in conversation. She resisted the impulse to lecture him, or to pity or condescend to him. From the outside it might seem that she did very little other than simply sit there in silence. In fact, however, she acted with responsibility, sensitivity, and faithfulness to her call and bore compassionate witness to Mark's process.

In her article, Jane Vennard invites us not only to practice being a compassionate witness, but to keep in mind the constant presence of that other, larger witness, which some might call God or the universe. This divine witness is ever-present and spiritual guides do well to remember that it is operative in every meeting. I often light a candle at the beginning of a session and say, "This is to remind us that there are three of us, here." The Divine is the ultimate compassionate witness—not judging or condemning or coercing, but through the gentle persuasion of circumstance moving us toward health and wholeness.

It might seem like this chapter is asking for a confusing number of shifts in perspective, and I think this is correct. It was utterly disorienting for the Buddha when his flash of *satori* came—when, for a brief instant, he beheld objective reality. This shift in perspective changed him utterly, and changed the world in his wake. As spiritual guides it is our responsibility to practice shifting our perspective. It is arrogant to think that we have it all figured out, that we know what is best for any of our clients, that our opinions, prejudices, or experiences are normative for our clients. A responsible spiritual guide, however, can, like Lucy, view her own opinions, thoughts, and fears with compassion, and yet intentionally shift perspective. Sometimes we can even gain a glimpse of the compassion with which the Divine views us.

Witnessing ourselves with compassion, witnessing our clients with compassion, and witnessing our session as the compassionate universe does requires patience and practice. It means having the humility to see that our perspective is limited, and opening ourselves to a larger reality that might challenge or frighten us. Since we often ask our clients to venture into scary territory, it is the least we can do. The bodhisattva resists the temptation to enter the place of safety until other beings can be safe. As spiritual guides, we are called to do no less.

5

Judaism, Ethics, and Covenants

Judaism begins with a covenant, a statement of ethical agreement, between a man and a strange new god. Abram lived in Ur of the Chaldeans, in lower Mesopotamia, so the story goes, probably around 4,000 years ago. According to the book of Genesis, the first book of the Jewish scriptures, known as the Torah, this god spoke to Abram and said, "I am God Almighty; walk before me, and be blameless. And I will make my covenant between me and you, and will make you exceedingly numerous" (Gen 17:1–2).

Abram was told to worship this god, and this god alone, and if he could do that, he would be blessed in an amazing way: this god would make the childless aging gentleman the father of a great nation, with ancestors "as numerous as the stars of heaven and as the sand that is on the seashore" (Gen 22:17). Abram was also promised a homeland for his people, to be revealed by the strange new god at a later time.

We aren't told if this was a difficult decision for Abram, but if any of us were to step into his shoes, it might be difficult for us. Abram was being asked to forsake the religion of his family and tribe, and to give up all the security of home and hearth to wander gods-knew-where, all because a little voice in his head told him to. Today, he might be prescribed an antipsychotic and told to try to forget about it; but fortunately for the people who became the Jews, Abram listened to the voice in his head, and took his family on the road. Due to his obedience, his name was changed from Abram, which means "father," to Abraham, "father of multitudes."

Genesis is full of stories of Abraham's adventures, and even though his new god seemed to be protecting him in the strange lands of his wandering, it didn't seem to Abraham that Adonai (or "the Lord," as the Jewish tradition prefers to call its god) was upholding "his" end of the bargain. When, Abraham wondered, would these promised children appear?

Abraham's wife, Sarah, seemed to be even more impatient than her husband about this particular issue. We aren't told whether she had a hard time pulling up the tent stakes and heading out into the desert, but we do know that being childless was a sorrowful burden to her. At some point she gave up on waiting for Adonai's help and suggested that Abraham take her servant Hagar to his bed, to have children in her name. Abraham agreed, and nine months later, Ishmael was born.

But then a strange group of visitors appeared at their camp, and promised that Sarah would give birth to a child. Sarah was eavesdropping on this conversation and laughed when she heard the absurd promise. Yet the promise came true in spite of her disbelief, and a baby boy was born to her. They called him "Isaac," which means "laughter" because she had laughed at the thought of such an old woman finally having a baby. Adonai had honored the covenant made with Abraham; Isaac was the first fruit of a great nation.

But now Sarah had a problem. Ishmael, the child born to her servant Hagar, had been born first, and Sarah wanted to make sure that her own child received the rights and privileges of a firstborn son. So she did a terrible thing, and convinced Abraham to banish Hagar and Ishmael. Tradition tells us that Ishmael became the father of another great nation: the Arab peoples, and the rivalry between these siblings continues even to the present day. Adonai had honored the covenant, but Abraham had not—yes, he worshipped only this one god, but his trust had wavered. As we shall see, trust is the foundation of any covenant.

This breach of trust created a problem for Abraham's relationship with his new god. The covenant was not broken, exactly, but the relationship had been damaged, and needed to be healed. Adonai decided to test Abraham, to see if he was willing to trust, once and for all.

Adonai exacted a terrible price to heal this relationship. Abraham was told to take his son, Isaac, to the top of Mount Moriah, and there to offer him up as a sacrifice. This sounds barbaric to us today, but human sacrifice was commonplace in the ancient world, and awful as it must have seemed to Abraham, it would not have been unheard of.

No one knows how Sarah took this news. My guess is, Abraham did not plan to tell her until after the deed was done. In any case, Abraham and Isaac began the long ascent up the mountain. Isaac asked him, "Where is the ram? What are we going to sacrifice?" Abraham must have choked on his own words when he replied, "Adonai will provide."

At the top of the mountain, Abraham bound his son and placed him on the altar. Just as he raised his knife to strike, an angel intervened and stopped him. Abraham had passed the test—he was willing to sacrifice his son in obedience to his new god. The trust that had been damaged was restored. Just then Abraham and Isaac heard the sound of a sheep bleating nearby. Sure enough, a ram was found with his horns entangled in the brush. Adonai had indeed provided.

The sacrifice of Isaac is an ancient story long revered by the Jewish people, but it is a problematic story. Who is this god that would demand such a cruel sacrifice—only to reveal that it had been a trick all along? It does not seem to be the action of a particularly moral being.

And indeed it was not. The notion of a moral deity would not occur to the Jewish people—or to any other peoples—for quite some time. Adonai—and the gods in general—were not seen as perfect. Israel perceived her god as being the source of both good and evil for quite some time. Why does Adonai need to explain anything to us? Adonai is God, after all, whose "ways are not our ways."

It is not just contemporary readers who have had difficulty with this story. Jewish scholars have struggled with it for quite some time. In fact, the memory of this struggle is so deep that it manifests in another early story involving Abraham's grandson.

Not only was Isaac not killed on Mount Moriah, but he remained true to his father's god and had two sons, Esau and Jacob. Jacob, in an act of deception, stole his elder brother's birthright, and fled into the wilderness to avoid the consequences of his trickery. While in exile, Jacob encountered an angel late at night. They wrestled until dawn, and Jacob refused to let the angel go until he got a blessing from him. This the angel does, but he also touches Jacob's thigh and wounds him. He also gives him a new name: *Israel*, "the one who wrestles with God."

Jacob (and by extension, the people of Israel who are his namesake) wrestles with the Divine and comes away with both a blessing and a wound. Thus begins an ancient tradition of contention with Divinity. Unlike some traditions, who would not dare to question Divinity, the Jews question their deity constantly. Not only is their god not perfect, but "he" can make mistakes, and even repents of his actions on occasion. [17]

This is a very healthy development, as it allows for real relationship between humans and Divinity. A relationship where one party is always right and the other party is always wrong is a dysfunctional one. Indeed, it is tyranny and not a true relationship at all. Between Israel and her god, however, we see a very real and touching relationship developing. Neither Israel nor her god is perfect. Both act in the heat of anger, both do things they are not particularly proud of. They hurt each other, they forgive each other, and the relationship endures. At this point, however, the covenant is an oral one—you might say they are still in the "dating" phase of their relationship. But that is about to change. The defining moment for the Jewish people occurs several generations later, in a foreign land—Egypt.

Jacob had twelve sons, one of whom was Joseph. Joseph had an uncanny ability to interpret dreams. These interpretations often depicted him being superior to his brothers, which caused no small amount of consternation. At last his brothers had had enough, and they sold Joseph to some passing traders and told Jacob he was dead.

Far from dead, Joseph was resold in Egypt, where he rose to power in a nobleman's house. The nobleman's wife tried to seduce him, and when rebuffed, accused Joseph of attempted rape. Joseph found himself in prison, where he found another opportunity to interpret dreams. News of his amazing ability soon reached the Pharaoh, who had been plagued by disturbing dreams of late. Summoning Joseph, he related the troubling dreams, which Joseph interpreted handily, warning the Pharaoh of an impending famine, and how to prepare for it. The Pharaoh put Joseph in charge of these preparations, and the young man became a prince in Egypt. When the famine struck, Joseph's own family was hit hard, and they moved to Egypt where Joseph's careful planning ensured there was enough for all.

People's memories are short, however, and the Egyptians soon forgot the debt they owed to these sons of Israel. Jealous of these rich foreigners in their midst, they eventually put them in irons and forced them to work as slaves.

For generations the Israelites toiled under the hard mastery of the Egyptians. And though they were far from their home, Adonai nevertheless heard them and acted to save them.

When the Pharaoh ordered all male children under two years of age put to the sword, a woman sought to save her son by hiding him in a basket and floating him on the Nile. The basket found its way to the Pharaoh's daughter, who raised the child as her own. This child was Moses, of course, and he was raised as a prince. His own heart was not as hard as the Egyptians', though, and in a fit of anger, he killed an Egyptian guard who was mercilessly beating a Jewish slave. Moses had to flee for his life.

He escaped into the wilderness where he encountered a local priest named Jethro. He married Jethro's daughter, Zipporah, and settled into a contented life as a shepherd. In his late middle age, however, the god of Israel appeared to Moses in the form of a burning bush, and revealed to him "his" true name.[18]

Adonai commanded Moses to return to Egypt to free the Israelites from slavery. Moses was not terribly excited by this plan, but after Adonai showed him some signs of "his" power, Moses finally consented, so long as he could take his brother along as a spokesperson.

So Moses and his brother Aaron went to the Pharaoh and demanded the freedom of the Jewish people. They were refused, however, over and over again. Each time they were refused, the god of Israel sent a devastating plague. In the end, the worst plague of all struck the land, the death of the firstborn sons of Egypt—a neat retribution for the slaughter of the firstborn sons of Israel a generation before. With the death of his own son, Pharaoh consented, and the Israelites fled.

Pharaoh, however, had yet another change of heart. No sooner had the Israelites gone than Pharaoh ordered his soldiers to bring them back. After all, one does not give up such a plenteous source of cheap labor without a fight!

Moses and the people were tempted to despair when they saw the Sea of Reeds on one side of them and the approaching Egyptian army on the other. It is there that Adonai performed one of the greatest miracles in the history of Western religion: Adonai parted the Sea of Reeds, and the people of Israel crossed as though on dry land.

The Egyptians tried to follow, but as soon as the last of the Israelites was on safe ground, the sea closed up and the Egyptians perished beneath the crashing waves. A Jewish myth says that as soon as they were safe, the Jews began to sing a song of praise; but when the Egyptians perished, the song shifted into a minor key and became a dirge. When asked why their song of joy and deliverance had changed into a song of mourning, Adonai replied, "Because my other children, the Egyptians, have just died."

Having won their freedom, the Israelites were a great, roving city in the desert without any system in place to govern themselves. Egyptian laws no longer applied, and there were no masters standing over them with whips to keep them in line. But Adonai was prepared to meet this need, too.

The god of Israel called Moses to the top of Mount Sinai and there gave him the tablets of the law—establishing a covenant that would endure for all time.

In this radical covenant, the god of Israel offered humans something they had never known before. Adonai was proposing something like a marriage between godself and the people of Israel. Adonai promised to be like a husband to them, and Israel would be like a wife to "him." This "marriage" is a motif that is repeated time and time again in the Jewish scriptures. The Song of Solomon is a love song that is not only highly charged erotically, but is also very moving in its portrayal of the deep affection between the lovers. These lovers have long been understood to be Adonai and Israel, a bold and novel tradition.

It is novel because up to that point, gods were almost always depicted as kings, and the people as slaves. It may be that the god of Israel was sensitive to this reality, and knew that Israel had had enough of slavery. Instead of treating them as chattel, Adonai offered them something no people had ever been offered before: a relationship of mutual commitment and responsibility—a marriage.

In every significant relationship, the parties involved must negotiate their commitments and boundaries. For a relationship to succeed, both parties must be clear about what will be required of them, and what they can expect in return. Thus Adonai proposed a covenant with Israel, an agreement about what Adonai expects of them, and what they can count on in return.

Adonai promised to be their god, to be faithful to them, to save them in times of trouble, to provide for them, to multiply them, and to give them a land "flowing with milk and honey" for their very own. To a bunch of refugees on the verge of annihilation in the desert, that sounded pretty good.

But what did Israel have to promise in return? In short, to worship no other gods, and to treat one another (including foreigners) with dignity and fairness. Just so there would be no confusion about what that entails, Adonai provided a detailed accounting of exactly what was expected of Israel in terms of governance, interpersonal relationships, ritual purity, and worship. The complex code of laws recorded in the Torah did not fall fully formed from the sky, but according to the biblical account, was revealed piecemeal in response to various crises Israel encountered in their first few years in the wilderness. With this code emerged a first in the history of human religion: the virtual deification of law, and the ability of humans, for the very first time, to know precisely where they stand in relation to their god. The law empowered the Israelites to feel secure in their dealings with their god and their neighbors. The boundaries were clear, as were the consequences if those boundaries were violated.

The boundaries were not arbitrary. Nearly every one had a defensible purpose, at least for the time it was given. The people were commanded to keep the Sabbath—not because there was anything particularly special about the seventh day of the week, but because humankind needs rest. People are healthier when they are not forced to work every single day without end.

This commandment to rest was another novelty, and it extended to all areas of Jewish life. Women were relieved from their household chores during their periods; fields were allowed to remain fallow one year out of seven; newlywed couples were supported by the community for the first year of their married life; and any slaves were to be set free every seven years.

These all sound like good sense. But what of those rules that boggle us today? The prohibitions against pork or shellfish seem arbitrary, yet make sense in terms of public health, for both can easily bear diseases (just think how far one would have to carry the shellfish in the desert heat to get it to the Israelites when these laws were given!). Prohibitions against homosexuality seem mean-spirited to us today, for whom overpopulation is an imminent reality, yet for a people whose very existence was so frightfully precarious it is easy to see how any union that did not result in children might seem frivolous and ill-advised.

Note that Adonai also has boundaries. No more would people tolerate the capricious whims of gods that threatened their vulnerable existence. Adonai promised to behave, and to protect them, and be true to them. This provided the basis of safety and trust in early Jewish society, and laid the foundation for both religious and civil society as we know it in the West.

It is significant that Adonai refers to this agreement as a covenant. A covenant is not the same as a contract. In a contract, if one party breaks the contract, it is null and void and neither party is bound to it any longer. But a covenant is different. In a covenant both parties agree to uphold their commitment even if the other party fails at theirs. Just as a husband and wife make a covenant to be faithful to one another, no matter what, Israel and her god entered into a similar arrangement.

This relationship of trust was soon to meet its first trial, however. Their god commanded the people to go into the land of Canaan and take possession of it. This sounded fine to them—until they heard back from the scouts they had sent ahead of them. They reported that the men were like giants, and that their military power was great. The people quailed at this news, and lost their nerve.

According to the Torah, this did not please Adonai one little bit. In fact, Adonai, who had already shown them more miracles than by rights any generation should see, took this lack of trust personally, and reacted more like an angry parent than a compassionate husband. Adonai announced that for their lack of faith the current generation would not, in fact, inherit the new land promised them. Instead, they would wander in the wilderness for forty years. Then their children would be given another chance to take possession of the promised land.

And possess it they did. After forty long years, and after Moses had passed away, Joshua led the armies of Israel against the city of Jericho. They marched around it seven times and blew their trumpets. In the panic that ensued inside the city, the inhabitants of Jericho killed each other, and the Israelites simply strolled in and took over.

These are the foundational stories of the Jewish people. Of course, the stories do not end here. The Jewish scriptures are filled with the tales of the fortunes and vicissitudes of the Hebrew people—of judges, priests, and kings who sometimes kept inviolate the covenant with Adonai (but more often did not). The people of Israel were even to become slaves again when they were conquered by the Persians in 721 B.C.E. This begins the famous "captivity in Babylon." It is here that the Jews came in contact with Zoroastrianism (more on that in another chapter) and inherited from that tradition a grand hierarchy of angels and demons, and a rich apocalyptic literary tradition. But the most important influence the Zoroastrians had on the Jews was their perception of Divinity itself.

It took a long time for the notion of "perfection" in Divinity to find purchase in human religion. Just as early Judaism did not see Adonai as perfectly moral, it also did not perceive Adonai as all-powerful. Before the exile in Babylon the Jewish people were not monotheists, but henotheists. Their god ruled only in Israel. If one journeyed into Babylon, one entered the jurisdiction of another deity, and was beyond the reach of the god of Israel. It was only when the Jews found themselves once again in a foreign land that they discovered—to their great surprise and relief—that their god was present with them there, too. Thus the god of Israel became God, the "Sovereign of the Universe," as Jewish prayers would forever after begin.

Eventually, Israel was allowed to return to their homeland, and to rebuild their temple. After the episodes of slavery in Egypt and Babylon, the Jewish people were understandably touchy about being under the control of foreign powers. The Seleucids conquered the region, and after sacking the temple in Jerusalem in 187 B.C.E., the people fought back. About twenty years later, the priest Judas Maccabaeus and his sons led a guerrilla revolt that threw off the yoke of the Greeks and restored self-rule (the Jews celebrate this victory at the feast of Hanukkah). Yet they were not able to keep out the Romans when that empire engulfed Israel, and their persistent resistance to the occupiers led to the utter destruction of Jerusalem and the temple in 70 C.E. In 134 C.E. Jews were banned from their holy city, Jerusalem, and they were scattered to the four winds.

They journeyed far and wide, to any country who would take them. With the temple system dismantled, they developed a new system of devotion centered on personal piety and devotion to the law. Rabbis ("teachers") rather than priests became the religious leaders, and a congregational form of communal worship evolved that survives to the present day.

The Jewish people are an anomaly in the history of humankind, in that any other peoples would have been assimilated into the cultures that they traveled to, yet the Jews, against all odds, retained their uniqueness and their identity wherever they went. Though they have been mercilessly oppressed and persecuted, misunderstood and murdered, they have through it all remained faithful to the sacred covenant they swore so many centuries ago to uphold.

Through it all, the Divine remained faithful to this people as well. This is not to say that Adonai's behavior was perfect—the god of Israel remained an emotional sort who often acted rashly. Yet there are those who remained faithful in spite of this (just think of Job, who lost everything yet refused to curse God and die). All this sordid history is testimony that covenant works. Even though it has been broken by one party or another, still the relationship endures. This is, I believe, yet another miracle.

Spiritual Guides as Covenanted Peoples

The image of Jacob wrestling with the angel—or with the Divine—is symbolic of the Jewish people as a whole. They are indeed a people who have wrestled mightily with Divinity, and like Jacob, have come away both wounded and blessed. This image is also useful for us who practice spiritual guidance. We wrestle with the Divine ourselves, and we bear witness to the wrestlings and struggles of those we companion.

Israel's wrestlings with Divinity felt safe and manageable because there were clear boundaries that both parties covenanted to respect. Even competitive wrestling can be done safely, but only if there are rules of the game in place. Spiritual guidance, too, has its own set of "commandments"— ethical covenants that protect both the spiritual guide and the client. These covenants form the boundaries that provide safe space for "god-wrestling" to occur.

Some of these covenants will be explicitly stated agreements between guides and their clients, either in word or in print. Others are implicitly agreed to when one deigns to practice spiritual guidance. Some are covenants between the guides and the Divine, and others are covenants one keeps between oneself and the larger community of spiritual guides. The closest thing to a "ten commandments" the spiritual guidance community has is the Ethical Guidelines produced by Spiritual Directors International, which can be found in appendix A. In the following pages we will discuss many of the covenants outlined in these guidelines, as they specifically apply to those practicing interfaith spiritual guidance.

A Covenant of Self-Care

Many of the commandments given to Israel concerned self-care, often spoken of as *mitzvoth*, or holy duties one is obligated to perform. The Jews were required to take appropriate time for rest and recreation—even animals and nonanimate entities such as the earth herself were provided rest. In the same way, spiritual guides must make sure that their own basic needs are met.

Adequate Rest and Recreation. All spiritual guides should make Sabbath rest a priority, regardless of one's spiritual tradition. Jews may rest on Saturday, and most Christians on Sunday. It does not matter which day you rest (unless it matters to your practiced tradition) so long as you can take one day of unstructured activity to heal yourself, find your center, and cultivate the interiority so necessary to our ministry.

In our go-go culture this is not an easy thing to do, especially if children or commitments to nonprofit organizations figure into the picture. Our culture does not encourage boundaries around busyness, and in fact, encourages busyness at every turn in a frenzied devotion to the god of productivity that has invaded even our religious institutions. Thus, setting and respecting such boundaries are our covenanted responsibility.

Proper Attention to Our Own Spiritual Lives. To help people on their spiritual journeys, spiritual guides must give proper attention to our own—it is hypocritical to do otherwise. Whether we follow a specific tradition, or if our path is eclectic and idiosyncratic, we still are responsible for our own spiritual growth, for the health of our souls. Spiritual guides cheat themselves and their clients if they are not actively working at their spiritual journeys, and actively engaged in spiritual community.

For most spiritual guides, this also means being engaged with one's secular community, neighborhood, and culture. Culture feeds our spirituality, and spirituality enriches and provides guidance for culture. Few people's spiritual journeys are divorced from the physical world around them. Unless one's spiritual path is that of the hermit, intentional dialogue between one's spirituality and one's community is essential.

Commitment to Our Own Spiritual Guidance. Of course it is also important to have a place to process one's spiritual life, to work out the tricky alchemy between spirit and culture, and spiritual guidance is by far the best tool we have for the job. Every person offering spiritual guidance should also have a spiritual guide of his or her own. It is unethical to practice if one is not being guided as well.

Though it is not ethically required, I also highly recommend being in personal psychotherapy in addition to spiritual guidance, as the two disciplines are highly complementary and each can quicken and enrich the progress of the other.

Commitment to Supervision. In addition to individual spiritual guidance, it is essential that every practicing guide be in supervision. Supervision is similar to spiritual guidance, but instead of focusing on one's spiritual journey, one processes with the supervisor the feelings and fears that arise within when sitting with clients. The focus of supervision sessions is not "did I do this right?" but "how did it make me feel when my client said this?" or "when my client said this, I felt all of this internal resistance," and the like. Supervision helps us to be better spiritual guides by focusing on our own processes as we sit with our clients. It's not about right or wrong, but about support, exploration, and the often necessary "reality check."

Supervision can take the form of either one-on-one meetings (which look very much like a spiritual guidance session), or it can be done in a peer group. In this model, many spiritual guides meet together—usually once per month—to check in about their practice and to support one another when group members need to process events that arise in their work.

Continuing Our Education. Just as one's ongoing need for support continues throughout one's ministry, so the need for continuing education persists as well. To practice ethically, a guide must keep abreast of contemporary theories and techniques being explored by the spiritual guidance community. This need can be met by reading professional journals such as *Presence,* published by Spiritual Directors International; going to lectures at regional SDI meetings; and attending workshops at the annual SDI conference. Networking informally with other spiritual guides is also helpful, as you can trade ideas and learn from one another's experiences.

Knowing When to Quit. Practicing ethically also means recognizing our own wounding and limitations. When Clara came to Jack for spiritual direction, the red flags were popping up for him almost from the start. Jack was raised Assemblies of God, and had spent most of his adult life trying to heal from the wounding he received from his conservative indoctrination. When Clara sat down across from him, she began the session by lamenting what a sinful country we lived in, and how God was going to cleanse it with fire. The atheists, cultists, and homosexuals were invoking God's most just wrath, she said, and she seemed to take great delight in the thought of the coming judgment.

A guide who was not triggered by such language may have been able to sit with Clara, to help her withdraw her projections and take responsibility for her own spiritual life instead of seeing herself as a victim in some cosmological war zone. Jack, however, as a recovering fundamentalist and a gay man, was simply incapable of sitting with Clara with any degree of distance or equanimity. Does this make Jack a bad spiritual guide?

If Jack had gritted his teeth and forced himself to sit through Clara's diatribes month after month, then yes, we should have some concerns with Jack's ability to be an effective guide for Clara. But instead of being masochistic, Jack listened as carefully as he could throughout the session. At the end of the hour he quietly and politely explained that he did not think that he was a good match for Clara, and recommended a couple of other guides who he thought would be able to companion her effectively. This was the most responsible thing for him to do.

In addition to noticing when a client triggers one's own wounding, one should be mindful of when a case is simply too far beyond one's comfort zone to sit with a client properly, or when a client's journey is simply too far afield from one's own area of expertise. For instance, a client that is exploring the Yezidis (a tradition often misconstrued as a form of Islamic satanism) may push you beyond both your comfort zone *and* your expertise. This is where networking is so important, as you may have met just the right person to refer such a person to at your last regional SDI meeting!

It is also important to note when you are carrying a full load of clients and cannot be fully present with any more. One should not have more clients in any given day than one can sit with comfortably, nor should one have more than one can keep straight mentally. Of course, one should keep notes on clients, but when someone steps through the door whom you know you've seen before but you can't even remember his or her name, it may be time to cut back.

You also must know how to say "no" when friends or business associates ask you to guide them. Spiritual guidance relationships are more fluid than psychotherapy relationships, but still caution must be exercised. We will talk more about boundaries a little later.

An important maxim in spiritual guidance is this: "When in doubt, refer them out!" There is no shame in admitting to yourself, your client, or your supervisory group that you might not be a good guide for such-and-such a person. This is not failure, it is just good, responsible spiritual guidance. Everyone has limitations, and we have an ethical obligation to ourselves to know when and how to say "no."

These are the covenants we keep with ourselves: to be kind and loving toward ourselves, to make sure we have adequate rest and playtime, to give proper attention to our own spiritual paths, and avail ourselves of adequate oversight. And, finally, to admit our own limitations without shame, and to practice responsibly within the boundaries of those limitations.

A Covenant of Care for One's Clients

Just as the law that Moses delivered to the people of Israel provided clear and unambiguous guidance for moral living, in the same way spiritual guides should provide clear and concise information about what the client can expect from spiritual guidance, and the guide's ethical commitments to the client.

Most of these can be made clear in an initial meeting, and some guides employ a written covenant for clients to read and sign before proceeding (see appendix B for a sample covenant). Whether this is covered in writing or orally, the following areas should be addressed.

Clarity about the Nature of Spiritual Guidance. Is the client clear on exactly what spiritual guidance is—and isn't? If you do not make this clear from the beginning, you will know very quickly, especially if your client treats his or her session as an opportunity to do psychotherapy, or in some other way wants to talk about something other than his or her spiritual life. If it seems your client does not want to stay focused on his or her spirituality, you may need to clarify the purpose and scope of spiritual guidance. They are paying for the time, but that does not mean they can use it in any way they like. It is the responsibility of the spiritual guide to keep the session focused and on track.

Of course, everyone needs a little latitude. It may be that your client is clear about what spiritual guidance is, but needs some time to warm up, or perhaps he or she typically comes to his or her point by circuitous routes. If so, be patient and walk that winding path with them. As Lao-Tzu says,

"If you want to be straight, allow yourself to be crooked."

Length and Frequency of Sessions. You should be clear from the beginning how long each guidance session will be. Do your sessions last one hour? An hour and a half? Is your hour a full sixty minutes, or is it of the "fifty-minute-hour" variety? Your clients will be fine with most any arrangement so long as they know what is going on.

How often will you meet? Many guides recommend twice per month for the first two months, then once per month thereafter. Seminarians and others who are working an intense spiritual program may need to meet twice per month or even weekly, depending on the severity of their process. If you can be flexible on this point, allow the client to decide how often he or she needs to meet.

The vast majority of clients meet once per month. If your client is not working an intense spiritual program and needs to see you every week, this is a red flag: your client probably needs psychotherapy, not spiritual guidance. If this is the case, you may need to do some clarification with your client to figure out just what sort of work is going to benefit him or her the most.

Compensation. Just as the Torah was very clear about how much the people were expected to contribute to their spiritual leaders, you should be equally up front with your clients about what you expect in the way of compensation. This is a very touchy subject in spiritual guidance circles. Not long ago I was asked to speak to a class on spiritual guidance. Another guide was also asked, and when she was asked what she charged for spiritual guidance, she responded that she did not charge for her services. "It is my gift to the community," she said with pride. Then all eyes turned to me and the same question was put.

"Well," I said, "I suffer under the possible misconception that my time is worth something and if you want an hour of it, it'll cost you $50." The debate between these two positions is far from over, and every spiritual guide needs to decide for him- or herself which way has the most integrity.

Most people who eschew payment are fortunate enough to have some substantial means of support—perhaps they are independently wealthy, or have a spouse that supports them. Most of us, however, have bills to pay and mouths to feed and simply do not have the luxury to give so much of our time for free. Some spiritual guides combine these approaches, charging those clients who clearly can pay, and balancing that with as much *pro bono* work as their schedule and budgets permit.

One thing to keep in mind is that we live in a consumer culture, and people simply do not value what they do not pay for. If your client receives guidance for free, he or she may feel free to simply blow off a "homework" assignment. But if that client has to pay for that time, he or she is going to want to get the most for the money, and will most likely honor his or her commitments. This might be a sad commentary on our culture, but that it is true cannot be disputed. If people value your ministry, they will be willing to pay for it.

While some guides may offer their services for free as a way of giving back to the Divine or their community, others may opt for this simply because they feel guilty receiving payment for such a "spiritual" enterprise. If this is the case, it needs to be addressed. The Christian scriptures tell us, "The laborer deserves to be paid" (Luke 10:7), and this is certainly true of spiritual guides. If this is a problem area for you, I have three words of advice: *get over it*. Our economy is based on currency, it is the measure of what we value, and it is necessary for your own survival. The work you do with your clients is going to be profoundly worthwhile for them and the vast majority of them will not balk at paying for your services. Most importantly, your time is valuable, your skills are valuable, and your ministry is valuable. *Get over it*.

Just how much compensation you will ask is entirely up to you. Most spiritual guides as of this writing (2005) charge between $25 and $70 per hour. Many guides use a sliding scale based on a client's income level. One system that works particularly well is to charge a dollar for every thousand dollars a client earns per year. For instance, if your client earns $25,000 per year, then their fee would be $25 per hour. If he or she earns $50,000 per year, the fee is $50 per hour, and so on. You don't need to see your clients' tax forms to verify this—it is best to trust them to pay you according to their conscience.

What happens if a client fails to show up for an appointment? This also needs to be spelled out at the very beginning. I usually give my clients one warning. After that, they need to pay for sessions missed. If a client begins to miss a number of sessions, even if they are not contiguous sessions, it needs to be addressed in the session. It may be that the client is experiencing resistance around subjects coming up in session and is having a hard time being present—literally. If this is the case, this resistance should be met head-on and addressed out in the open. Resistance is a sign that good work is being done, difficult as it often is.

It may also be, however, that your client is simply being irresponsible or is not valuing the work you are doing together. His or her commitment to the work may be wavering. This, too, needs to be addressed directly. It is important that your client understand that simply not showing up for an appointment is deeply disrespectful of you and that in a relationship of mutual reverence such as spiritual guidance, such disrespect will simply not be tolerated. You may need to discontinue sessions with such a client. Or it may be that just threatening to discontinue will snap him or her out of it, and help your client realize what he or she has been doing. Or, more likely, he or she will simply choose to discontinue the guidance relationship. If this is the case, a guide should not try to talk him or her out of it. When and if the client is truly ready for spiritual guidance, he or she will return, either to you or another guide.

Closure. Every relationship with a client comes to an end sometime, and it is important to let them go with grace. For many guides, a client may come to fewer than five sessions before terminating the relationship. A guide should not see this as a failure in any way. It is just the way things go. It very well may be that such a client got exactly what he or she was needing in those few sessions. Or it may be that he or she discerned that you were not a good fit for him or her. This is also normal, and we need to be careful not to let our egos get involved in these decisions. Only the client can truly say whether or not he or she feels sufficiently comfortable with you to do his or her work (of course, you get a say in whether or not you feel comfortable working with him or her, as well).

Another thing that should be made clear in the very beginning is for how long you expect to meet. If the client is a student, you may agree to meet through the end of his or her semester. Or if the client needs help with one particular aspect of her spiritual life, you may agree to meet for three months and then to reevaluate the relationship. Most guidance relationships, however, are open-ended, and continue so long as the client is committed to the process, or so long as he or she is deriving benefit from the sessions.

It may be that a client will work with you for a few years, and then discern a need to switch spiritual guides. This, too, is entirely normal. Everyone has a style and limitations; everyone has only so much to offer a client. If the client perceives that he or she has done as much good work as he or she can with you, and wants to try things out with someone else, the guide must not perceive this as a rejection or take it as a personal insult. Our clients are the experts on their lives, not us. It is their decision to make, and we need to allow them to follow the guidance of the Divine that comes to them, even if we strongly disagree with their decision to do so.

Most spiritual guides prefer to do an "exit" session with clients who are discontinuing. If this feels too invasive or threatening to your client, it may be best to just let it go. But if he or she is willing, it can be very helpful to the client and to you. It is a chance to recap where you've been and where you are now, to appreciate the good work you have done together, and to celebrate the partnership you have enjoyed. It is also a time for the client to clear the air, to offer some constructive feedback on your guidance style, or to discuss anything that might have been painful for him or her. This is not a time to defend yourself or to justify your methods. This is a time to hear the client's truth and to be as present with his or her feelings as humanly possible in that moment.

You can cry, wail, argue, and defend yourself later with your supervisor, where it is appropriate for you to process your feelings about the session or your client. In the exit session, however, the focus must be on the client and everything he or she says must be held in love, even if you are about to blow a gasket on the inside.

A Covenant to Guard the Dignity and Confidentiality of Your Clients

In the Torah, Adonai demands that the rights and dignity of all people are defended—especially those at risk such as widows, orphans, foreigners, and others who might "fall through the cracks." All were to be cared for, and their dignity maintained. Those of us offering spiritual guidance today are likewise obligated to guard the dignity of our clients, especially since many of them come to us in their most vulnerable moments.

Honor Your Clients' Beliefs. Though it may at times be difficult, it is imperative that we honor the beliefs, values, and conscience of our clients. Spiritual guidance is not an opportunity to fashion people in our own image, and our own path is rarely the right one for anyone else. Therefore it is very important not to project our own beliefs, values, or opinions onto our clients. We are not here to change their beliefs, but to deepen their experience of connection with the Divine.

Often, however, it is clear that certain beliefs are destructive or are themselves an impediment to spiritual communion. This, however, is not really our call. It may be that through discussing a clients' beliefs, a client may come to this conclusion by him- or herself. When this happens, it is often a graced moment. But we must be very careful to follow Lao-Tzu's advice and *follow* in this area, rather than lead.

Also, questioning a belief that may be limiting to the client is not the same as attacking his or her theology. Precisely where to draw that line, though, is tricky. Ricky was raised in Conservative Judaism, and did, in fact, consider himself to be quite conservative religiously. He told his spiritual guide, a very liberal Jew named Kate, that he did not pray except at synagogue, because "God has better things to do than to listen to me." Kate disagreed with almost everything Ricky believed, yet she was not triggered by his rigidity, and was able to sit with him where he was. Kate had many choices as to how to approach Ricky's case. She could have tried to convince Ricky that it is part of the Jewish tradition to reevaluate itself in conversation with culture in every age, but that would have been violence to Ricky's spirituality.

The notion, however, that "God has better things to do than to listen to me," seemed to her to be a nonessential belief that was limiting his connection to the Divine. She questioned this assertion, and using traditional Jewish spirituality to reinforce her arguments, she told him that God wanted nothing more than to hear Ricky's prayers. Ricky confessed that, aside from the synagogue service and Shabbat prayers, he really did not know how to pray. This was a major revelation for him, and opened a new way ahead for his spirituality. He continues to practice Conservative Judaism, but his prayer life is flourishing for the first time in his life.

Spiritual guidance is not an opportunity to proselytize clients, to convince them that our theology is superior to theirs, or to destroy someone's faith, even with the intention of building it back up with something "healthier." Spiritual guidance should never be used to enforce doctrinal conformity, even if we are practicing under the auspices of a specific religious community. Such approaches are violence, and they betray the essential trust that is the foundation of the spiritual guidance session.

Do Not Exploit Your Perceived Power. Spiritual guides should have no power over clients whatsoever. Clients must come of their own free will, and they must be free to discontinue their sessions whenever they choose. There must be no repercussions, no shunning, no threats involved. Yet even if there is no real power that a spiritual guide has over a client, there is often a *perceived* power differential between the two. The client may perceive the spiritual guide as an authority figure, and afford the guide greater authority in his or her own imagination than the guide actually possesses or, hopefully, even wants. A power differential that is real in a client's imagination is real, period. A spiritual guide who exploits this power differential, however unfounded it may be, also betrays his or her clients, no matter how benevolent the intention.

A person who has any control over a client whatsoever should never, under any circumstances, serve as this person's spiritual guide. One should never try to direct one's employee, family member, or anyone else where a real or imagined power differential in another arena may impact the spiritual guidance session.

A teacher may conceivably serve as a spiritual guide, but not if that teacher is responsible for evaluating that student, or if the teacher may in any way influence the success or failure of the student. Therefore, if one is asked to be part of an evaluation committee for a student who you also serve as guide, it would be best to decline this responsibility. If in doubt about any case, it is always best to raise it with a supervisor or one's supervisory group.

Maintain Proper Boundaries. You could say that the whole of Jewish Law is nothing more than a system of boundaries governing every part of human life. Human beings need boundaries to function socially and ethically, we even need them for our own self-esteem, for we do not know what to think of ourselves without some external guidance as to right and wrong.

Recognizing and respecting boundaries is essential in maintaining an ethical practice of spiritual guidance. Our boundaries are not as rigid as they are for psychotherapists, but they are not as casual as social relationships, either. There are some absolutes (such as not directing those you have power over, as just stated above), but other boundaries will need to be established according to your own comfort level.

It is normal to guide someone who is a fellow member of one's own faith community, but it is not okay to guide a personal friend with whom you have a social relationship outside of the guidance relationship. A pastor or rabbi may guide a parishioner, but only in those communities where such leaders have no administrative powers or responsibilities, or may not in any way negatively impact the life of the client if the relationship sours. One should also avoid directing friends of clients.

Becky was a spiritual guide from the Zen Buddhist tradition, whose client, Zoe, a Unitarian Universalist, was very excited about their sessions together and often spoke about them to her friends. Zoe's friend Allyson decided to give Becky a try, and made an appointment. Allyson was also a Buddhist, but studied with a Theravadan teacher who often denigrated other schools of Buddhism. Allyson parroted her teacher's opinions in her direction sessions with Becky, who found the criticisms of her own spiritual path annoying. She felt defensive and the negativity between herself and Allyson quickly escalated. Allyson decided that Becky was a charlatan and when she discontinued her sessions, she pressured Zoe to do the same. Zoe resisted, but ultimately was unable to maintain both relationships due to Allyson's vehement opposition. After a couple of months, she ended the relationship with Becky, who was understandably distraught over the succession of events.

It is tempting to receive referrals from current clients, but as Becky's case demonstrates, it is rarely wise.

One should also be careful with regard to bartering. While for tax reasons, or when a client is financially limited, bartering can seem attractive, one must use it with caution. I have one client who is handcrafting ornate tote bags in her spare time. She charges $150 for each bag, and is doing a brisk business at craft fairs and boutiques. My mother, grandmother, and ex-wife would thrill to such beautiful handiwork, and in exchange for spiritual guidance, every three months, she delivers another bag. Christmas will definitely be easier this year.

But not all bartering arrangements are as clean-cut as this one. For many months I exchanged spiritual guidance for bodywork with one client. After a couple of sessions of bodywork it became clear to me that material was emerging that I felt uncomfortable revealing to my client. I took the situation to my supervisory group, who recommended that I discontinue either spiritual guidance with this client or the bodywork. Fortunately, my client was a mature and wise soul who understood the dilemma and the recommendations of the supervisory group. She gave me a referral to a trusted colleague in the bodywork field, and we continued to do spiritual guidance together.

Every situation will be different, and everyone will find themselves now and then in dual relationships that feel uncomfortable. When this happens, it is best to describe the situation to one's supervisor or supervisory group. One should not hesitate to do this out of shame or the fear of judgment. Supervision is not about judgment, but about guidance, which one should be humble enough to avail oneself of at every opportunity!

Respect Confidentiality. It is essential for the success of your sessions that your clients feel safe. A large part of that safety is knowing that anything that is stated within the guidance session *stays* in the guidance session. Confidentiality is not just an ideal, it must be a rock-solid reality. All it takes is one slip, one piece of gossip repeated to a trusted friend or loved one in a moment of carelessness to utterly ruin not only one's client's but one's own reputation.

Just as binding as the seal of the confessional for Catholic priests, the expectation of confidentiality is likewise sacred and immutable for spiritual guides. Information given in a spiritual guidance session may never (with very few exceptions, which we'll get to in a minute) be repeated to anyone. In spiritual guidance we encourage our clients to be as real as possible, to be vulnerable and honest. Often they tell us things they have never told another living soul, sometimes they say things they've never before admitted even to themselves. This is a holy, tender, and fragile bond of trust that must never be betrayed. Without this trust, the practice of spiritual guidance is impossible. One has not only one's own reputation to guard, but the reputation of this ministry as a whole. The importance of this particular boundary cannot be stressed strongly enough.

That being said, there are situations in which confidentiality must be broken. If a client poses a danger to him- or herself or others—such as threatening suicide, or threatening to kill or injure someone else—one is ethically obligated to break the confidence of a client and notify the proper authorities.

Whenever this happens, one should tell the client of one's intentions to inform and to invite him or her to participate in the process. Regardless of the client's response to this, one must follow through on reporting the danger. In fact, failure to do so will open one up to legal repercussions.

Other situations where one has a legal duty to warn authorities include the suspicion of child or elder abuse, or the abuse of a disabled person, and circumstances where one has foreknowledge of a crime that has not yet been committed. One may also be required to report spousal abuse if one is working in a hospital or hospice situation.

One may also have to break confidentiality if a court subpoenas a client's records. In such cases it is best to consult an attorney to protect both you and your client. Such cases are rare, but in our increasingly litigious society, they will become more and more commonplace as the ministry of spiritual guidance continues to expand into the mainstream of spiritual life.

Clients should be informed of your commitment to their confidentiality at the outset of your relationship, along with the rare circumstances in which such confidentiality may need to be breached. Talking about such things up front will help clients feel secure, reinforce for them your commitment to good boundaries, and will protect you in extenuating circumstances. You may even want to include such information on your intake form.

At times it may be useful to converse with a client's psychotherapist, pastor or rabbi, or other helping professional, so that you can coordinate your efforts, get a reality check, or seek an outside perspective on your client that may be helpful to you in your sessions. To do so, you may ask your client to sign a consent form that will give you permission to discuss confidential information with specifically named professionals. They will probably also insist on their own consent forms being signed. This protects everyone involved, and can often be very helpful indeed. A sample of such a form can be found in appendix C.

Finally, one can respect one's clients' confidentiality by keeping records of every session safe, in a place where they cannot be casually observed by others or easily stolen. For added protection, I only identify my clients by first name (and the initial of their last name where I have two or more of any first name).

Confidentiality is also problematic when one is doing guidance via e-mail. E-mail is by its very nature public, as anyone with a little hacking know-how can intercept and read private e-mails. If you decide to do spiritual guidance via e-mail, you must be sure that your client is aware of the dangers of this practice. E-mail is usually safe—I have been doing it for

years without an incident. But there is always the possibility—just as there is
the remote possibility that someone could bug your office. So long as your
client is aware and agrees to the practice, you should be fine.

Finally, it is important that guidance sessions be conducted in a place
that feels safe enough to your client to truly open up. It is important to make
sure that conversations cannot be overheard when the door is closed. You
must ensure not only the illusion of privacy for your client, but the reality
of it as well.

There are exceptions to this, of course. If your client prefers meeting out
of doors, in a park, a restaurant, or other public place, then he or she will be
aware of the possibility of things being overheard. I mention this because
almost everyone encounters a client now and then for whom "creative"
meeting spaces are helpful. So long as you and your client have a discussion
about the pros and cons of your agreed-upon meeting space with regard to
privacy, you can proceed with confidence.

A Covenant with Your Colleagues

Just as we have responsibilities for our clients and own spiritual lives, so we
also have responsibilities to the ministry of spiritual guidance at large, and
the many colleagues who practice this ministry. We can only speak of the
"spiritual guidance community" if it truly is a community, which requires
participation and commitment. It is important to attend local gatherings
of spiritual guides, and, if possible, larger national or international gatherings as well. Spiritual Directors International has a fine network in place,
many regions of which have very active monthly or bimonthly meetings.
Involvement in such gatherings is important for continuing one's education and for mutual support. It is also important to know who is practicing in your area, and what their strengths, weaknesses, and specialities are.
You never know when you will need to refer someone out, and knowing
who is in your area will go a long way in making sure you refer people
appropriately.

As you increase in experience and skill, you will find that you have much
to offer people who are just beginning in the ministry. Regional gatherings bring together people who need mentors and people who are ready to
mentor others in the ministry. Spiritual guidance is an exceedingly social
ministry, and you will find that as your circle of friends and acquaintances

in the ministry expands, so will your opportunities for personal and professional growth.

Finally, as already touched on above, it is important to reiterate that we have a responsibility to practice ethically for the protection of our colleagues and the ministry as a whole. Spiritual guidance is rapidly gaining in popularity, and so far we have an excellent reputation. Protecting the integrity of this ministry should be a major priority when wrestling with the many ethical dilemmas that inevitably arise.

Protecting Ourselves and Others

The Talmud tells us, "If a man draws near the fire, he derives benefit; if he keeps afar, he is frozen, so with the words of the Torah: if a man toils in them, they are life to him; if he separates from them, they kill him" (Sifre Deut 143a). The fire in this verse represents safety, warmth, and comfort. As anyone who has ever been lost in the wilderness on a cold night can attest, being near the fire is life.

Just as the Torah—the scripture recording the covenants of the Jewish people—kept Israel safe, so the Guidelines for Ethical Conduct issued by Spiritual Directors International provide safety and comfort for us and our clients. When we stray from them, we wander into dangerous places.

These guidelines are not contracts: they are binding on us even if our clients do not hold up their end of the bargain. Nor are these guidelines laws—spiritual guidance is not a legally regulated ministry—at least not yet. We should hold them with more reverence than mere laws. Laws are broken every day, even by most of us in insignificant ways. But we must remember that we hold the souls of our clients in the palms of our hands, and that responsibility is an awesome and terrible one. We fail them—and ourselves—if we take it lightly.

6

Zoroastrianism
and Discernment

An old Iranian myth relates that the Soul of Creation was in distress at the evil abroad in the world, and begged the Creator to raise up from among the community of human beings a deliverer who would correct religious errors and inspire people to cooperate with the divine plan.

The archangel of Righteousness and Truth, called Asha, agreed that such a savior was required, and she lent her voice to the entreaty. But she added that this savior should be among the mightiest of mortal souls in order to have every chance of success.

The Creator heard their complaint, and complied, nominating a lowly but righteous Vedic priest named Zarathushtra. The Soul of Creation and Asha the Archangel were *not* pleased. "Why, O Wise God, did you choose this man? He is righteous, but he is weak. He is not a king commanding armies, he has no worldly power to speak of; how can he possibly accomplish the task you have set before him?" But the Creator rebuked the Soul of Creation and the Archangel. "What is needful here," he informed them, "is not worldly power, but spiritual power, and Zarathushtra is indeed blessed with such spiritual potency."

Both divine beings instantly acquiesced and admitted that, of course, the Creator knew what he was doing, and entreated him once more. This time they asked him to give Zarathushtra the mental and spiritual strength he would need to fulfill his mission. The Creator agreed, and bestowed upon

Zarathushtra the supreme spiritual power, which would also be a hallmark of his teaching: the power of discernment.

The Prophet

Born in Persia around 3,000 years ago, the Prophet Zarathushtra was of priestly lineage, and given the name Spitma. Many years before, when the Aryans, the horsemen from the Russian Steppes, rode on their conquering mission south, some of them went to the east into India, and brought with them their tribal religion, which we now call Vedism. This religion mixed with the native traditions of India and became the primitive Hinduism immortalized in the Vedas, the oldest collection of Hindu scripture. Some of these horsemen, however, went west, and settled in Persia (modern-day Iran, Iraq, and Afghanistan).

Like their brothers in the East, these invaders were also followers of the Vedic religion, speaking a language very similar to Sanskrit, and worshipping a vast pantheon of deities representing the many forces of nature. Early Vedism required many complicated and elaborate rituals, and a priestly caste emerged to satisfy the hunger of the gods. Spitma was born into just such a family, and he was an ardent student of the priestly craft.

But at some point, Spitma became disillusioned with the Vedic religious system. The hierarchy was hopelessly corrupt, and seemed to exist more to extend the ambitions of the royalty than to satisfy the gods. And what mortal person could tell the difference? Spitma could, and it was in the midst of his disillusionment that the Creator spoke to him, and he was overcome with holy wisdom.

The Creator gave Spitma a new name, "Zarathushtra," which can translate into English as either "The Golden Light" or "That Guy Who Owns the Yellow Camel." Old Persian Vedic, despite its similarities to Sanskrit, is a difficult language to decipher. When the Greeks later encountered the followers of Zarathushtra, they transliterated his name as "Zoroaster," which has been used interchangeably by scholars to refer to the prophet ever since.

A New Religion

Just as it was necessary for Hinduism in the East to undergo reforms to address the corruption that plagued it, Zarathushtra was chosen as the agent of the Vedic reformation in the West. But the solutions that he came to differed substantially from those his brethren in India would devise, and his innovations would dramatically affect the trajectory of Western history.

Like the Hindu reformations, his insights shifted the polytheism of the Vedic system to a variation on monotheism, but of a very different kind. As we have seen in chapter 3, in Hinduism's Upanishadic shift the many gods of the Vedic pantheon were revisioned as being one God with an endless number of faces. Thus the Vedic heritage was honored and reinterpreted in light of the new monotheistic revelation.

In Zarathushtra's formulation, however, there was only one God, whom Zarathushtra called Ahura Mazda, "The Wise God." But what to do with all the rest of the deities of the Vedic heritage? Zarathushtra discerned that these were not gods at all, but an array of lesser divine beings forming a vast hierarchy, each in the service of Ahura Mazda. These beings mirrored in heaven the earthly hierarchy of the monarch and his many governors.

Thus, Ahura Mazda was served by seven immortals, or archangels: Spenta Mainyu (the Creative Holy Spirit), Vohu Manah (Good Mind), Asha (Righteousness and Truth), Kshathra (Kingdom and Justice), Spenta Armaiti (Devotion and Serenity), Haurvatat (Wholeness), and Ameretat (Immortality). Three of these immortals are male, and three are female. Spenta Mainyu alone is androgynous.

Serving below these immortals were untold numbers of other divine beings, called Yazatas ("Adorable Ones") each of whom had responsibility for some aspect of the natural world. These beings were not worshipped by the followers of Zarathushtra, but they were revered—a difficult distinction for people even in the best of times. Nevertheless, in this way, the old Vedic system of hundreds of gods was revisioned. Each god and goddess still had his or her place, but each had undeniably suffered a demotion. There was only one God, Ahura Mazda. Everyone else was a servant, albeit an angelic one.

But just as Hindu Vedism recognized that the gods had opponents, the demons, Zarathustra likewise acknowledged that Ahura Mazda was not unopposed in his rule of the universe. An eighth divine being, Angra Mainyu ("Evil Spirit"), embodies the evil at work in the world. Over time, followers of Zarathushtra envisioned this being as having at his command legions of demons, creating an inverted hierarchy to counter Ahura Mazda's.

Nothing was created evil in Ahura Mazda's universe, however. All things are good until and unless corrupted by Angra Mainyu and his evil spirits. All beings, especially human beings, have free will, and all have the responsibility to choose between good and evil. But in such a complicated world, where there are few absolutes, how does one distinguish what is good and what is evil? The ability to discern between the two became the primary spiritual discipline in Zarathushtra's religion, and an ingenious system of discernment was developed to help people in this task (more on this later).

Eventually Zoroastrians came to see the universe as being pitched in a great cosmic battle between these two forces: Ahura Mazda, the Good and Wise God, and Angra Mainyu, the Evil Spirit bent on destroying everything that is good and holy. The earth is the battleground, and no one is exempt from the conflict. Everyone must choose sides. Either you are fighting for the good, or you are fighting against it. There are no neutral parties.

An elaborate body of literature resulted from this mythology, which we today call "apocalyptic." This literature dramatically depicts, often in fantastic and surreal imagery, the cosmic battle and how it will reach its climax. Of course, Ahura Mazda will be victorious, but it is just how this victory will be achieved that keeps the reader enthralled.

Zarathushtra's Exile

As you might expect, when Zarathushtra began preaching his new revelation, it was not well received by the religious establishment of his day. He and his meager band of followers were roundly denounced and, in fact, driven from their homes. But Zarathushtra trusted Ahura Mazda, and stepping out on faith alone, led his disciples into the wilderness. There they wandered in search of a place they could safely call home, a place that was hospitable to their peculiar religious message.

Finally, after many hardships, they came to the small kingdom of Balkh in modern-day Afghanistan. Kavi Vishtasp, the king of Balkh, heard of Zarathushtra's message, and invited him to his palace to preach. The king was captivated by the prophet's eloquence, his message of justice, the importance of spiritual discernment, and the relative simplicity of his cosmological system. Against the angry protests of the country's established priests, the king embraced Zarathushtra's teaching. He rebuked the priests for their arrogance, and set up Zarathushtra's system as the state religion.

Zarathushtra's troubles were not over, however. He had found a welcoming home for his followers, married a local woman, and fathered many children. He had found a royal patron to protect him and promote his teachings, but his battles with the priests of the old religious establishment would dog him for the rest of his days. Indeed, he was murdered by a remnant of the old priesthood many years later, when he had reached the ripe old age of seventy-seven.

The Influence of Zoroastrianism

His vision did not die with him, of course. Zoroastrianism spread quickly beyond the small kingdom of Balkh, and eventually became the dominant religion in the Middle East. As such, it could not help but influence other religious movements that came in contact with it. This is nowhere more evident than in its profound effect on Judaism.

In the year 721 B.C.E., Assyria conquered Israel, and deported many Jews (described in the Jewish scriptures in 2 Kgs 17). Later, in 597, the Babylonian empire conquered Assyria and removed the Judean nobility and much of the Jewish population to Babylon. Since this was a largely Zoroastrian empire, the Jews found themselves surrounded by Zarathushtra's wisdom, and this contact changed Judaism forever.

As we saw in the last chapter, prior to their removal to Babylon, the Jews were not monotheists, but henotheists (different gods have jurisdiction over specific territories). In Babylon, the Jews discovered, to their great relief, that the God of Israel was with them even in a foreign land. There they encountered Zoroastrian monotheism, and adopted its vision of one God ruling over the universe as their own.

They also encountered the great libraries of the Zoroastrians, and the reverence with which the followers of the prophet regarded their scriptures. The Jews began writing down the oral wisdom of their own tradition, and thus it was in exile that most of the Jewish scriptures were actually set down in writing and compiled.

Prior to their exile, the Jews had no concept of angels as we think of them today, and certainly none of demons. Once more the religious legacy of the Zoroastrians was adopted, and postexilic Judaism was both blessed and cursed with complex hierarchies of celestial and infernal hosts, along with detailed descriptions of their abodes, Heaven and Hell.

The writings of the Zoroastrians, read and studied by the Jews in exile, resulted in new genres of religious literature previously unknown to the Jewish tradition. Apocalyptic literature such as is found in Daniel, Ezekiel, and the pseudepigraphal writings became increasingly popular, and sometimes depicted the God of Israel's wrath against the Zoroastrians themselves.

The contact with Zoroastrianism rendered Judaism not unrecognizable, but certainly dramatically changed from the faith the Jews had known before; and they bequeathed these theological innovations to another religion having its origins in the Middle East: Christianity.

Without the Zoroastrian influence, Christianity as we know it would not have existed. With no literary legacy, no Heaven or Hell to reward or punish people, no angels to help us or demons to hurt us, no judgment day with its sheep and goats, no climactic battle at the end of time, Christianity would have emerged a very different animal, if indeed it emerged at all.

Zoroastrians even figure prominently in the stories of the birth of Jesus, since the three wise men were undoubtedly Zoroastrian priests, who had discerned signs in the stars of a new king soon to be born, and hurried to greet him. When the Persians later conquered Judea, every church in Bethlehem was burned to the ground except for one: the Church of the Holy Nativity, no doubt because the devout Zoroastrian soldiers could not in good conscience burn down a temple with a carving clearly depicting three Zoroastrian priests over the doorway.

Zoroastrianism's Decline

Zoroastrianism reigned for a thousand years as the state religion of three Iranian empires. By the seventh century c.e., however, the final empire was on its last legs, and when the Muslims began to invade, the people embraced Islam and the less oppressive rule of the imams. After all, Islam was not that different from Zoroastrianism, and in fact, honored Zoroastrians as "people of the book" along with Jews and Christians. They both honored prophets sent by the one God, and Zoroastrianism had bequeathed to the Muslims, via Judaism and Christianity, much of Islam's cosmology and theology.

Some people remained faithful to the revelation of Zoroaster, however, and in the tenth century they fled their Islamic invaders and settled in Western India. Known as the Parsis (literally, "Persians"), this tiny band of Zoroastrians is the only living pocket of this once-great religion, and they have been influential far beyond their numbers not only in India but also in England, the United States, and everywhere else there are communities of Parsis today. There are currently about 150,000 Zoroastrians in the world, and they continue to be shining lights in science, entertainment, and politics.

While they continue to influence the world, the Zoroastrians' greatest influence came at the height of their power, when the unprecedented teachings of a rejected prophet changed the trajectory of world history. I believe this was not only due to the innovative cosmology Zarathushtra taught, but because of the importance placed on the primary spiritual discipline he pioneered: spiritual discernment.

What Is Spiritual Discernment?

Zarathushtra's example contains much for us to benefit from. He teaches us that the most important religious activity is not exterior—whether rituals are performed correctly, what words are used in prayer, what one wears to worship, what one eats, etc.—but instead that it is the interior process—of discerning light from darkness, good from evil, proper and improper—that most concerns Divinity.

Furthermore, Zoroaster took the locus of religious activity away from the professional caste of the clergy, and put it directly into the hands of the common people. Whereas before one's religious standing was determined by how many rituals one could afford to have performed on one's behalf, and on whether or not these were performed perfectly by the priests hired to do it, a Zoroastrian measured the success of his or her religion by how faithfully one went about one's daily business. They asked themselves how the simple decisions made every day helped or hurt the cosmic struggle in which we are all engaged, and how the most subtle of discernments sometimes have universal impact—taking responsibility for such decisions with great prayerfulness and deliberation.

Today we do well to consider our seemingly mundane deliberations with such caution and prayer. Not long ago, I sat with a client who was noticeably distraught over whether or not her vote had helped tip world events into war. At first I thought her concern irrational, even obsessive. But as I listened to her sincere grief and regret over what she thought then to be an ill-considered and irresponsible exercise of her civic responsibility, I felt sad that more people do not take their own political discernments so seriously.

Zoroaster correctly recognized that the faithful practice of discernment is at the very heart of spiritual life. Nearly every moment presents us with choices, most of which we make on the fly, without a moment's hesitation. As my client above taught me, a bit more soul-searching is almost never a bad thing. And for those of us serving as spiritual guides, it accounts for a large part of what we do.

Exactly how we frame our discernment will differ by necessity according to the spiritual paths and needs of our clients. Traditional believers will be concerned as to whether or not they are living in a way that is in line with the divine will, and will focus on a source of external authority to help them decide. Spiritually eclectic folks will be more likely to ask whether or not they are living from the center of their integrity, which is sometimes a more difficult method of discernment in that it draws primarily on an internal authority whose wisdom might itself be a challenge to discern. Though the language and imagery surrounding these questions are very different, the meat of the matter is very similar indeed: Am I living in the right way? How do I know, and what do I do about it?

Many traditions have developed systems to help people make such essential discernments. The balance of this chapter will focus on a few of these methods: cognitive, revelatory, divinatory, emotional, and somatic, each of which are instructive to us as spiritual guides, and each of which may prove useful for one or another of our clients.

Cognitive Discernment

The first method to be considered is probably the most common one employed by spiritual directors, and it was also the method taught by Zarathushtra himself. As we have seen, Zoroastrians are very concerned with making choices that will assist Ahura Mazda in his battle for the fate of the universe, and eschewing those things that would in any way give Angra Mainyu the upper hand. In Zarathushtra's language this was known as discerning the "Good Mind."

Since everything in the universe was engaged in this conflict, one could not be sure that even the simplest of decisions did not somehow carry cosmic consequences. In reacting against what he perceived as the magical—and often corrupt—practices of the Vedic priests, Zarathushtra devised a method that was very down-to-earth, and which invested great responsibility in the individual believer. This method honored both reason and intuition, and in so doing, provided a built-in balance between internal and external authority.

The first step in Zarathushtra's method was *observation*. Zarathustra entreated his followers to make a disinterested analysis of a situation, to attempt (to the best of one's ability) to see it from all sides. This is always good advice, as there is usually more than one side to any conflict, and our ability to extend empathy—to walk a mile in another's shoes, as the saying goes—can go a long way to diffusing charged situations. Sometimes our own pain or outrage blinds us to the larger picture in the light of which our own suffering is revealed to be a result of a misunderstanding, an unfortunate inevitability, or simply inconsequential relative to the pain of another. Zarathushtra entreats us to get out of our own skin long enough to see how others involved are affected, to empathize with other perspectives.

As soldiers in Ahura Mazda's army, believers' own situations are subservient to the ultimate end—the fateful battle for the universe—and their own tribulations and complaints are often revealed to be petty or irrelevant when seen against the backdrop of eternity. This is no less true for us today. Though we may chafe at the militaristic imagery, we can still take the sentiments to heart. Whatever ultimate fate for the universe we may envisage, it can serve as a reality check for the mundane conflicts we contend with day in and day out. "How important is this from the perspective of eternity?" is often a humbling question, and can sometimes defuse a momentary feeling of rage or resentment.

The second step in Zarathushtra's method is the *application of reason*. Once we have the full "lay of the land" of a situation, we are empowered to make an intelligent analysis of it. We can usually predict logical outcomes of various plans of action, which can help us weigh the values of our actions. We can rationally make decisions regarding the delaying of our own gratification, and how our decisions might impact those around us. In elevating reason, Zarathushtra was by no means advocating a method for intellectual elites, he was instead investing rare trust for a religious leader in the deliberative powers of the average person. Every person, both female and male, rich and poor, noble and common can be trusted to read the situation at hand and make responsible decisions.

These first two steps in Zarathushtra's method are active, the locus of this activity residing within each individual believer. The next two steps, however, hand the results of these two steps over to the Divine. The third step is *meditation*, and as in other traditions, it demands we be quiet and listen for the divine whisper. In the previous steps we've thought about the problem at hand, but step three asks us to stop thinking about it, and simply *be* with it.

This results in the final step, *intuitive knowing*. In the quiet of meditation, we create space for new information—indeed, inspiration—to arise. This stage asks us to pay attention to what thoughts, insights, revelations, images, feelings, fears, or warnings arise within us. This may very well be the voice of the Divine speaking to us about our problem, and requires some trust that if we are quiet, the Divine *will* speak.

Joseph did not know about Zarathushtra's model, but his spiritual director did. When he came to his regular session with Elizabeth, he was highly anxious. He had just been offered a job in another state, which would pay much more than he was currently making. Unfortunately, the move would take him away from his ex-wife and children, who were very much settled in their northern California community.

He had been round and round the problem, and could find no happy answer. "What does Spirit want me to do?" he asked Elizabeth, and she could see in his eyes a bit of desperation. He looked like he had not been sleeping well, and she was not surprised. He often shared in his sessions about his children, who, though in high school now, were still a big part of his life.

After hearing a full explanation of the situation, Elizabeth asked if he had talked to his kids and ex about the move. And what had they said? He said his ex had encouraged him to go, since his child support payments would be easier to sustain (his record with this had been spotty in the past). His children had shrugged and said, "Whatever. Can we come stay with you in Arizona sometimes?" His feelings had been a little hurt that his children seemed not to care whether he stayed or went, and his ex just seemed eager to be rid of him.

Then Elizabeth asked him to separate himself from the emotions he was feeling, and to approach the matter logically. Besides his children, what ties kept him in northern California? Joseph loved his Course in Miracles group, but he knew he would find another study circle—he was thinking of moving near Sedona, after all. Most of his closest friends had already moved themselves, and he could stay in touch with them as easily in Arizona as he could now. Then there was his current job, which he truly loved. Sure, it didn't pay much, but he was very fond of his co-workers and felt a great deal of pride in his job. "If it didn't work out in Arizona, could you come back?" Elizabeth asked. "I don't know—probably," he answered. Sure he could; he was very good at what he did.

Next Elizabeth suggested they spend some time in silence to bring the matter before Spirit, and to ask for guidance. After Joseph had been silent for about five minutes, Elizabeth asked him quietly, "As you sit in the presence of Spirit, what thoughts or feelings arise in you? What images do you see, what words do you hear?" After another five minutes or so, Elizabeth could see that Joseph had tears in his eyes. "What did you see? What did you hear?" she asked. "I saw the sun rise over distant mountains, and I heard Spirit say, 'The desert is a place of healing.' But I argued with the voice, and said, 'What about my children?'" He was still trying to get a grip on his emotions.

"What did Spirit say to that?"

"It said, 'You are your father's son.' My dad was often gone on business trips. I missed him, but I knew he had to go to provide for us. I always want-ed to do things differently." In the end Joseph decided to go, but he and Eliza-beth spent several sessions talking about the grief he felt over leaving behind his children, and his own unfinished grief regarding his father. Though there was work to do, he felt a sense of peace once he had made the decision. And his children *loved* going to Arizona.

Zarathushtra has given us a model that is amazingly intuitive: when we are faced with a discernment to make 1) we try to view it from the perspective of others; 2) we apply our powers of reason; 3) we meditate; and finally 4) we listen for a word from the Divine. This model honors our internal authority, while still encouraging us to be open to the wisdom of the Divine. It models for us the balance between empowerment and humility that all good discernment requires. Zarathushtra's method may be ancient, but it is still one of the best, and also one of the most comfortable and intui-tive for us in the West.

Revelatory Discernment

As you may recall from our chapter on native traditions, indigenous peoples do not generally believe in a "fall of humankind," and therefore see no essential divide between humans and the natural world. Human beings are as much a part of the world as the trees and animals are. Evil in these systems is not seen as "rebellion" against some deity or another, but simply as being out of harmony with the rest of nature. Native religion is concerned, then, not with eradicating evil, but with restoring harmony where it has been lost, and sustaining it once it has been achieved.

Unlike later Abrahamic traditions, which pictured humanity as being essentially at war with nature, native traditions assume that everything in nature is benevolent toward us, and is, in its own way, useful to help restore and sustain harmony. Even demons in native traditions are working to restore balance, serving in their own peculiar fashion to frighten us away from that which is unhealthy for us and to drive us toward that which will restore us to peace. In native traditions, the world is good and can be trusted to help us in our discernments.

Native traditions often employ a method of shamanism, in which a journey is made into another world—sometimes called the Otherworld, Faerie, or the Dreamtime, depending on the specific tradition being considered—and in this other place wisdom is gleaned that may help us understand what is happening in our own world.

In our own day, Michael Harner has done much work to educate people about the shamanic method of discernment, which is a revelatory model. In journeying to the Otherworld (or by employing a shaman to journey on one's behalf) one seeks revelation—the revealing of wisdom from a spiritual source.

To journey to the Otherworld, one must achieve an altered state of consciousness. This can be helped by meditation, drumming, or by the use of various psychotropic plants, such as soma, ayahuasca, peyote, or cacti. Zarathushtra railed against the use of soma in his own time, and there is certainly reason for caution, as such substances can be frightening to the uninitiated and have the potential for abuse. Yet when used by experienced shamans in a ritual context, they can be useful tools indeed.

In some traditions, the journeyer has the option to travel to the Upper World, make a "lateral move" to the Middle World, or go down to the Lower World. The creatures one may expect to encounter differ in each place. The Upper World is heavenly, bright, and noncorporeal. As Sandra Ingerman describes it in her wonderful book, *Soul Retrieval*, "I know that I am standing on something but am often unsure what is holding me there. . . . I might come across . . . a lake . . . or a city of clouds. Power animals live here, as well as teachers in human form."[19] Power animals are spirit guides in the form of animals that can talk to us, and are one of the most important sources of wisdom for the shamanic journeyer.

The Middle World, by contrast, is much like ours, but still exists in a nonordinary reality. Time can be stopped there, and parts of people's souls can be trapped in a certain time when a trauma happened to them. Such moments can be visited in the Middle World and reengaged. Great healing can occur here.

The Lower World must be reached by going down into the earth, either through a cave or a tunnel. Unlike the Upper World, there is nothing incorporeal about this place. The ground is solid, the rocks are hard, the water is wet. The beings encountered here include power animals, spirits of nature, and some human beings who have deep connections to the earth.

On one of my own journeys, I struggled over how to discern what are my own likes, dislikes, and feelings, and which are those of my parents. I was raised in a very conservative evangelical environment, and often did not feel at liberty to have opinions of my own. This has caused a lot of distress in my adult life, as I have chosen a very different path in many ways from my parents. But what, I wondered, were my own feelings, and how many were simply reactions against my Fundamentalist religious formation? I decided to take the matter to a shaman.

As she drummed, I descended lower and lower into the underworld. Eventually I reached a cavern with a stream flowing through it, lit with lots of colors just like the many caves I had visited as a child. I sat zazen in the cave for a few minutes, until my power animal emerged from the back of the cavern.

He is an enormous black panther, with shiny, silky fur and a disconcertingly surly demeanor. I explained to him what I was trying to discern, and without any warning whatsoever, he lunged for my belly, sank his teeth in, and pulled forth from me a huge, tangled mass of different-colored yarn.

Knocked flat on my back, it looked like my guts were spilled out all over, only much more colorfully than one might imagine. The panther hovered over me for a second, and then set to work. Using his nose, teeth, and especially his paws, he began sorting the yarn by color. He gathered together a large bunch of yarn that was either black or dark brown, and yanked it out of me. Once it was free, he coiled it like a whip, and set it to one side. Then he continued sorting, using his claws like combs. At one point he found another, smaller group of black threads, and yanked those out, making a smaller coil about the size of my fist. This he also set aside, and went back to sorting.

Eventually he had succeeded in sorting all of the yarn spilling forth from my belly by color, bound each color together, and then stuffed them all back in. I don't know how he did it, but he sealed me up and then sat back on his haunches like he was waiting for a treat.

When I sat up and faced him, he handed me the large coil of dark yarn. "What's this?" I asked. "That's your connection to your parents," he answered. "You can put it in a drawer, hang it on your wall, whatever you want. The point is, it's no longer inside you. You will make your own decisions from now on."

Then he handed me the smaller coil, "This is your connection to God." I took it, and turned it over in my hand. I understood him to mean that it was my connection not to the real God, but to the God of wrath I had been raised with.

"What do I do with this?" I asked him.

"Give it back to God," he said flatly.

I realized that I would have to return to the surface soon, so I decided to use my time with him as wisely as possible. "Why are you so surly?" I asked him. "Are you mad at me?"

"I'm not mad," he said.

"Then why so curt, so unfriendly?"

He turned and padded away into the recesses of the cavern. "The world is hard," he threw over his shoulder, and then was gone.

That journey was truly life changing for me, as I have found myself growing more fond of my parents since it happened, less threatened by their judgment, becoming more of my own person.

Shamanism isn't always so dramatic in its results. Very often the wisdom one gleans leads to more questions than answers, and the answers given are sometimes maddeningly obscure. Yet to the degree that such information helps us to consider the matters at hand from other angles, in more creative ways, it can be enormously helpful. The elders and power animals aren't about to tell us what to do, but they are very good at giving us pieces of a larger picture that invariably have bearing on our discernments, if we are open-minded enough to make the connections.

Divinatory

Also arising from native traditions are various practices of divination. Like shamanism, these methods seek assistance from a seemingly external authority; though from a mystical perspective, this distinction may be specious. Still, it *feels* like the wisdom is coming from somewhere—or from someone—else.

Divination usually employs some apparently random assemblage of items, which can be "read" to reveal meaning for the discerner. The native African Yoruba tradition uses the casting of cowrie shells. How they fall gives information that the questioner or the priest can interpret.

In China, the I Ching is used, in which hexagrams are generated using the casting of coins or sticks. Each hexagram describes a topological feature that bears some metaphorical relation to the matter at hand.

In ancient Europe, animals were used. Sometimes the entrails of sacrificed animals were "read," while later traditions "read" the tracks left by foxes in a specified and consecrated lot.

Native traditions are not the only ones to use divination, however. The ancient Jews cast a special pair of "dice" called the Urim and Thummim. When not in use, they resided in the breastplate of the high priest, but when important discernments needed to be made, they were removed and cast to determine the will of God.[20] Likewise, the Hindus and Zoroastrians were skilled astrologers, finding causal relationships between the movements of the stars and earthly events.

These are not simply the superstitions of primitive peoples, as the modern mind-set has for so long dismissed them. Indeed, they can be very powerful and helpful partners in one's discernment. How they work is a mystery. Is it the spirits speaking? Is it a manifestation of Jung's synchronicity? Or is it simply a tool for helping us make creative connections we otherwise would not have made, to see things we would not have noticed?

I choose to be agnostic on such questions, but I have been oftentimes amazed at the appropriateness of a tarot reading, and have found comfort in the mysterious images of the I Ching. Indeed the tarot has probably become—along with astrology—the divinatory means of choice for West-erners. While many people consider it a means of telling the future, others are rediscovering the tarot as a discernment tool. Gail Fairfield's wonderful book *Choice-Centered Tarot* is an excellent example of this renewed focus.[21] One very simple method she employs requires drawing three cards, face up. The first card represents one's present situation. The second card represents one's attitude toward the situation. The third card signifies the main thing one should keep in mind. In this way the cards do not tell us what is going to happen, but do help us see more sides to the situation than are readily apparent.

There are nearly as many divination methods as there are tribes and nations, as divination is fairly ubiquitous in human culture. Far from being nonsense to simply be discarded, as modernity would have us believe, divination is a vital discernment tool that can be used even within one's spiritual guidance session.

Benjamin is a Wiccan priest who has a small practice in spiritual guidance. Betsy phoned him late one afternoon and asked if they could have a session later in the week, as she was in some distress. When they met, Betsy looked close to tears. "I'm pregnant," she told him. "And I don't know what to do. Should I have the baby? If so, should I keep it? What does God-dess want me to do?"

They talked about fertility, one of the most important concepts in their religion, and whether or not it was proper to impede it. Benjamin pointed out that Wiccans don't usually have a problem with nonreproductive sex. Sexual pleasure is a joyous end in itself, and one need not feel guilty if no children result from it. Indeed, Betsy had long used birth control, yet it all seemed different once the seed was planted and she found herself with child.

"I've gone round and round with this, and I just don't know what to do." Her boyfriend was not ready to commit, and indeed, she had not even told him yet. No need, she thought, if she was not going to have the child. But every argument yielded an opposite argument that seemed equally valid, and her head was spinning. Sensing this, Benjamin said, "Let's do a tarot reading."

Betsy drew three cards, using Fairfield's method. The first card, the present situation, yielded the King of Pentacles. This card depicts a satisfied-looking king on his throne, holding a pentacle. "What do you make of that?" Benjamin asked.

"Well, usually the King of Pentacles represents someone who is intelligent, competent, someone who is sufficient to . . . meet what is coming." She stopped, and blinked back tears for a moment. "Maybe this is telling me I'm enough—I'm smart enough, strong enough to handle . . . *motherhood*." The word seemed strange to her.

The second card, representing her attitude, yielded the Tower. The card depicts a large tower being struck by lightning, and two frightened figures falling from it. "Yup," Betsy said, "That's me all right. Terrified that I'm just going to be falling to my own destruction."

Benjamin smiled compassionately at her, and drew the third card. "This is what you should keep in mind." He turned over the Ten of Cups. The card showed a couple in loving embrace looking toward the sky where there appeared ten cups spread out along a rainbow. Two children play near the couple's feet. "The card of contentment," she whispered. "It's going to be okay, isn't it?"

Benjamin laughed. "Oh, Betsy. You are an amazing woman. No matter what you decide to do, you are going to be all right. I think the reading is simply affirming what you already know."

"I think I've been so blinded by fear . . . ," she smiled at him. "So the question is, what do I really want?"

Betsy had been paralyzed by her anxiety, but reassured by the affirming reading, she was able to break through to the real issues involved. After a few more sessions, she decided to keep her baby, and has not been sorry since.

Emotional

Another method utilizes the emotions as a discernment tool. This method was devised by Ignatius of Loyola, a soldier born to a noble Roman Catholic family in sixteenth-century Spain. He was wounded during a siege in 1521, and suffered a very long and difficult convalescence. As he lay in bed, he found himself fantasizing to pass the time. Soon, however, he noticed an odd thing about his fantasies. He discovered that when he fantasized about the life he longed to return to, a life of luxury and the glory of battle, he was entertained, but was left feeling hollow and dissatisfied. When, however, he fantasized about living the life of one of the saints he had been reading about, a strange peace descended upon him, a peace that did not seem to fade. He thought this curious, and he began to pay close attention to his feelings as he thought and daydreamed. Eventually he came to realize that his fantasies and desires were leading him to God.

When he was well enough, he journeyed to Monserrat, where he made a formal confession to a priest. When he was finished, he hung up his sword at the altar of the Blessed Virgin Mary, and traded his clothes for a beggar's. He then entered a monastery at Manresa where he had many mystical experiences. There he began to develop his famous *Spiritual Exercises*, a book that has been a mainstay of Catholic spiritual formation ever since.

The *Spiritual Exercises* gives instructions for a month-long retreat, in which participants withdraw from the world and are led in a series of guided imagery journeys. In each of these meditations, the participant vividly imagines him- or herself present at a scene drawn from the Gospels. After the meditation, the participant processes by him- or herself the feelings and ideas that emerged, and later, discusses them with a spiritual guide.

What Ignatius had discovered lying on his sickbed was that his own desires and feelings were not evil, as so many preachers throughout the ages have testified, but that if they are truly listened to and given proper attention, they can lead to the place of greatest integrity for us.

Spiritual guides can learn much from Ignatius's example. Few of us are very aware of what it is we *really* want, and that is what this method does for us: it helps us sort out what we *think* we want from what we *actually* want in the place of our most authentic knowing.

The key to this system seems disarmingly simple: to pray for what we desire, and then pay attention to what happens. It usually happens this way: We think we know what we want, and we pray for that thing. Then we pay attention to the feelings that emerge as we pray from day to day. Ignatius speaks about a "spirit of consolation" and a "spirit of desolation" that emerge from our prayer. We would probably use less spiritualized language today, and simply ask, "How do you feel when you pray for what you want? Do you feel depressed or comforted?"

Sometimes the feelings that emerge are surprising, for as we continue in this process, we may find that the things we thought we wanted were simply pointing to deeper desires that are even more true for us. Then we may realize that the things we really want are not the things we thought we wanted at all.

Wim arrived at his session obsessed with the notion of getting married—in fact he spoke about almost nothing else. At their next session, Maggy, his spiritual guide, invited him to pray for what he wanted, so Wim started praying in earnest for a wife. As he did, he realized what he would have to give up if he got married: his career (he worked many long hours), and his autonomy. As he went deeper with his prayer, he realized that what he really wanted was to be loved. This led him to pray for himself, and he began to journal about the many ways he did not feel loved as a child, and eventually he began to journal about how he did not feel lovable as an adult. As he stuck with the process, he discerned that he never felt loved by his parents, or even by God. As he began to pray for this kind of love, his focus shifted. He realized that marriage wasn't what he was after at all, and he began to pray that he could love himself and feel loved by God. His obsession with marriage dissipated quickly as he discovered the true desire behind the obsession, and was able to bring this true desire to the Divine.

This kind of discernment goes on and on, as, like an onion, layer after layer of desire is peeled away to reveal our true needs and wants. Far from being hedonistic or selfish, praying for what we desire can truly lead us to wholeness and integrity as we discover who we really are and what we really want.

Somatic

Yet another tool for discernment is the body itself. Most of us have had the experience of the body acting independently of the mind in order to safeguard our health. I went through a period last year when I was working so hard that I hadn't had a day off in nearly four weeks. I was running here and there maniacally, trying to fulfill all of my obligations (and to do them all perfectly, of course). Finally, my body simply had enough of it, and came down with a massive cold that had me in bed for a week. It was exactly what I needed, and I have not forgotten the lesson.

My body knew what it needed, and when I wouldn't give it what it required, it simply took it, which proves that it is wiser than my mind. This is often the case, which we can use to good effect in session. Just as Vajrayana Buddhism honors the body as a fast track to enlightenment, so spiritual guides can often check in with the body to get a quick "read" on a situation.

Focusing was developed in the 1960s by psychologist Dr. Eugene Gendlin as a way to bypass the conscious mind and tap into the wisdom that resides in the body. In this method, a spiritual guide may ask a client where a thought or a feeling or a situation resides in his or her body. Based on the information that emerges, the body can often tell us something that the conscious mind either does not know or is actively (if subconsciously) resisting.

Further work was done in this direction in the 1970s by Peter A. Campbell and Edwin M. McMahon, who termed their method BioSpiritual Focusing. Simplifying Gendlin's model, they suggest the following steps. First, ask yourself, *What most needs to be listened to inside me?* Pause to notice what this is, and where it appears in the body. Next, ask yourself *how it feels to be with this information.* If it feels safe to be with it, ask, *Is there an image, a word, or a feeling that relates in some way with what is happing within me?* If such a thing emerges, *notice how it feels in the body.* If nothing comes, or if you must wrap up before the process is complete, ask, *How do you want me to care for you until we can speak?* When finished, *note how you feel* compared with how you felt before you began. *Savor the feelings* you notice, and *give thanks* for them.

This seems like a lot to remember, but the method can become second nature with some practice. And, of course, rules are meant to be broken, and these are only guidelines that can help us in this work. One must also be open to the nudging of the Divine that can interrupt the process or take it in another direction.

Focusing is often very helpful indeed. Lee stepped into my office like she always did, a little late. I had always felt her ambivalence about coming to session; often we talked about whether she should continue. Her persistent lateness was, I thought, her body betraying this ambivalence. This session, though, lent us the opportunity to seek more such wisdom. She talked about how restless she had been in synagogue lately. She was glad for the liturgical demands for standing up at various points in the service, because if she had to just sit there, she said, "I'd go crazy."

"Honest to God, I'm worse than my kids. And it doesn't set a good example."

"What's this restlessness about?"

"I don't know. And I've tried everything I can to control it. I avoid caffeine before service, I make sure I've gone pee—" she laughed; "I do everything I tell my kids to do! But it's no use. Just sitting there is hell."

We talked about it some more, but seemed to be getting nowhere. Eventually I suggested we check in with her body about it. She was open to the idea.

"Why don't you close your eyes, and get grounded . . . relax as much as you can . . . just sink into your body, and be as aware of it as you can. When you think about the restlessness, where do you feel it in your body?"

She wiggled uncomfortably, and then spoke haltingly, "I feel it in my butt."

"What do you feel?"

"Pain."

"Pain?" She nodded. "Stay with that for a minute, and make sure that's right . . . " I waited, and she cocked her head like a dog for a moment.

"Pain," she said with certainty.

I moved into the questioning step. "What would cause your butt to hurt?"

"The only thing I can think of was . . . well, that was where my Dad used to beat me with his belt when I had done something wrong." She opened her eyes and they looked cloudy and troubled.

"Lee," I said, leaning in, "Are you feeling guilty about something?"

She burst into tears. It wasn't so much a *shift* as an *avalanche* that lasted a full five minutes. "I had an affair with someone at work," she confessed. "It was only one time, about three weeks ago, and it's over. But . . . ," and she looked away and wept.

"Thank you for trusting me enough to share this with me."

"Well, I wasn't planning to! You jerk." She laughed through her tears. "But I'm glad I did. Thank you."

Using the Focusing method, we can access not only things the mind is not conscious of, but even material someone would rather not engage with in session. The body does not lie, despite the most earnest efforts of our minds to do so. Special training is available in Focusing and BioSpiritual Focusing through numerous schools and spirituality centers, and I highly recommend it, as this is such a subtle and rewarding method.

Other Methods

Of course, this does not exhaust the list of discernment methods. The cognitive, revelatory, emotional, divinatory, and somatic methods are just the tip of the iceberg. Other methods to investigate include mythological/archetypal, dreamwork, heuristic, ecopsychological, and many many more. Not every method is going to work for every client, nor is every spiritual guide going to feel comfortable with every method. What is important is to have a variety of methods with which one is familiar and comfortable ready and waiting in one's "toolbox" to be pulled out as needed.

Zarathushtra's insistence that we pursue the Good Mind, that we be adept at sorting good from evil, is as important for us today as it was for his early followers more than 3,000 years ago. Fortunately for us, it is not something we have to do alone. Indeed, such discernment comprises a large portion of what we do in the practice of spiritual guidance.

7

Christianity and the Wounded Healer

The sun shone hot on the Judaean countryside as the pilgrims poured out of Jerusalem. Some of them rode on donkeys, but most of them were on foot. They had heard that the prophet, John, was preaching and baptizing nearby, and were eager to catch a glimpse of him. Some of them even wanted to follow him.

There was a great deal of unrest in Israel. The people chafed under the yoke of Rome, and many believed that the temple priesthood had sold out and was actively collaborating with Rome. Feeling betrayed by their spiritual leaders, people were hungry for a voice that sounded authentic, that truly spoke for God.

John was already a legend. Born into a priestly family, he rejected the life appointed to him, and pronounced judgment on the established system. He had gone off to live in the wilderness, surviving on a meager diet of locusts and wild honey. Dressed in animal skins and a wide leather belt, he seemed a madman, proclaiming that the day of Israel's deliverance was at hand. "Make straight the way of the Lord!" he cried, and people flocked to him. There were the curious, the true believers, and those who desperately wanted to trust that John was right. Yet there was no evidence that Rome's stranglehold on their country was loosening—how could their deliverance be even close?

John was preaching a message familiar to them—their occupation was due to their own unfaithfulness. Just as the Jews had been carried away into Babylon to punish them for their spiritual infidelity, he said they were being punished again for the hardness of their hearts. Just like Isaiah and Jeremiah before him, he warned them that continuing the way they were going would only bring more trouble.

The only way to save Israel, he preached, was to repent, to soften their hearts and change their ways. He stood on the riverbank and addressed the crowd gathering on a hillock nearby. As more and more people arrived he scolded, cajoled, teased, and mocked them. Those listening to him did not know whether those saying he was mad were right, or those who insisted he was a prophet of God.

He implored them to wade into the river, and be baptized as a sign of repentance. Some did; most, however, sat restless on the hillside, still unsure what to think. After about an hour, no more were coming. The recently baptized gathered on the far side for instruction. John pleaded with the crowd. None stirred.

Then from over the hillock, a voice arose. "I'm ready." As the man came into view, John shaded his eyes to see, and was shocked to recognize the man as his own cousin, Jesus, from Nazareth. "Look, everyone!" John shouted, "This is the lamb of God, who takes away the sins of the world."

When Jesus was close enough to speak normally, John deferred to him, saying, "You should be baptizing me. I'm not worthy . . . "; but Jesus insisted, and John led him into the water, and baptized him while the people watched breathlessly.

As Jesus came up out of the water, the clouds parted and a dove descended upon him. Some thought they heard a voice, rolling as if with thunder, "This is my beloved son, listen to him!"

The people could not believe what they were seeing, what they were hearing. Suddenly, the name of Jesus of Nazareth was on everyone's lips. They knew they had witnessed something important, but they were not sure what it meant. Some of them took the words the voice spoke to them to heart: they listened to him. They began seeking him out to hear him teach. Some of John's own disciples asked leave to abandon the prophet and follow Jesus. John felt a stab of resentment, but swallowed it quickly. "Of course," he granted them leave. How could he do otherwise? He, too, had heard the voice.

Soon after, Jesus disappeared. He was led by the Spirit of God into the wilderness, where he faced the same trials and temptations common to all people with power. Though tempted sorely, he resisted assuming power over nature, over other people, and over God. The result of this time was a clarification of vision, a purification of soul, and a new sense of mission. John was right, the blessed kingdom that Israel had waited for so long was indeed at hand. In fact, it was already here.

Returning from the desert, he assumed the mantle of a Pharisee teacher of the law, a rabbi, and began teaching in earnest. Soon a small band of students formed around him, some of them were John's disciples, some of them he sought out himself. He chose twelve of them to share his life, to be his most intimate and trusted companions. But there were others; women began to follow him, to the horror of those steeped in social propriety. Others came, and soon Jesus was assured a small crowd wherever he stopped to preach.

But the people were not only intrigued by the content of his teaching, they were also troubled by it. They all wanted to hear about the coming kingdom of heaven—about how God would send an anointed one, a great and holy king, to ride into battle against the Romans. They wanted to hear about how this anointed one (*messiah*, in Hebrew) would defeat Rome's power, and put asunder their empire; how he would set up a new throne in Jerusalem, and how all the gentile nations who had persecuted and tormented them would kneel before their own terrible and righteous king, who would rule them with justice. The people wanted to hear about how they would have their day, they wanted to know when it would finally arrive. John had said their vindication was at hand, and they flocked to Jesus hungry for hope.

But though Jesus spoke about what the kingdom of heaven was like, they were disappointed that his teachings were so short on details. When would the armies be raised? Who was God's anointed king, and when would they see him? When would the big battle commence?

But when they asked him these questions, Jesus cocked his head like a dog, as if they were speaking another language. "The kingdom of the Father is spread out upon the earth even now," he told them, "and people do not see it."[22]

His listeners scratched their heads. Whatever could he mean by that? Jesus never spoke to them about armies or battle strategy—and he always dismissed such talk when his disciples asked him about it privately, much to everyone's consternation. Some began to grumble.

Indeed, there was much to object to in their rabbi's teaching, and some of it was beginning to bother the temple priests and the other rabbis as well. He was telling people that God did not care about people's social stations, that those who were the lowest of the low would have the places of greatest honor in heaven, and that those who rule on earth would be servants in the hereafter. He also cursed the hypocrisy of his fellow Pharisees, and once his anger got the best of him, and he drove all of the businessmen out of the temple court using a horsewhip.

He was making enemies among the powerful elite, but he did not seem concerned about it when his disciples warned him. The poor people, for their part, loved him, and it was their thoughts, feelings, and needs that he seemed most concerned about. He touched the untouchables, healed lepers, lame people, and the blind. People began calling him a miracle work-er; yet it was the people's own faith, he insisted time and again, that had healed them.

The poor had little education, but he did not talk down to them. He had come from a working-class family himself, and he knew that what people loved most and remembered best were stories. So he told a story about a man who had been robbed by bandits and cast to the side of the road to die. A temple priest saw the man, but didn't want to get his hands dirty, and passed by quickly; another holy man did the same. Finally, a Samaritan—the enemy of the Jewish people, and a heretic besides—saw the man, and took pity on him and helped him. And the people learned that God wanted them to love their enemies, to treat them with the same compassion they would hope to receive themselves.

Jesus told another story about a man with two sons, one of whom couldn't wait to make his way in the world, and begged his father to give him his in-heritance early. The young man took his money and blew it all on wine and women. Hitting rock bottom, he returned to his father to beg his forgiveness and to offer his service as a slave in return for food and shelter. But instead, his father wept with joy to see him, put an expensive robe over his shoulders, and called for a party to welcome home his lost son. And the people understood that no matter how far they might roam, God weeps with joy when they return with a whole heart, and holds nothing against them.

Some of them started to get it: the kingdom of God was not a political nation that would soon be erected by the sword, it was an interior state of grace that was present and available to anyone who had the eyes to see it, to anyone who would exchange hatred for love, enmity for friendship, privilege for the common good.

But as his love of the poor grew, the contempt in which his fellow religious professionals held him grew in direct proportion. Those with political designs were likewise disaffected—it seemed that Jesus was not only not planning to overthrow Rome, he was indifferent to it. In fact, they noted with horror, he treated the Roman soldiers with the same kindness and compassion he treated everyone else, healing the servant of one, and dispensing advice to others.

An organized resistance to Jesus' teaching began to form. His fellow Pharisees sought him out and tried to trap him into performing some act or propounding some teaching that could be grounds for legal action. When Jesus healed a man on the Sabbath, they confronted him, yet he countered them saying, "If one of you has a child or an ox that has fallen into a well, will you not immediately pull it out on a Sabbath day?"

They thought perhaps they could get him in trouble with Rome, and so they waited until a crowd had gathered, including some centurions, and then asked him, "To whom does this money belong?" Any rabbi worth his salt would say it was more important to tithe to the temple than to pay the Roman taxes. Even the centurions pricked up their ears to hear how he would handle it. But he saw through their ruse and cleverly asked them, "Whose likeness is on this coin?" "Caesar's," they answered. "So," he said with a twinkle in his eye, "Give what belongs to Caesar to Caesar, and give what belongs to God to God."

More confounding than any other action, however, was Jesus' habit of going for dinner with almost anyone who asked him. It made sense that a poor, itinerate preacher would welcome a meal whenever it was offered, but many of his co-religionists had very clear rules about whom it was proper to share a table with. At that time, for a rabbi to sit down at dinner with someone carried great meaning. A meal is a sacred thing, and for a rabbi to share one with someone meant that he approved of them, and implied by his actions that God approved of them as well. Thus, Jesus outraged his fellow rabbis when he regularly sat down for dinner with political traitors, nonreligious people, even prostitutes. By doing so he was saying to these unrepentant sinners, "I approve of you, and God approves of you, too."

It was all too much. The rabbis did not see that in doing this, Jesus was showing them the love and acceptance that God felt for them as well. The last straw came when Jesus told a man, "Your sins are forgiven you." The religious leaders felt that finally, they had caught Jesus in a fatal error. Who was *he* to forgive sins? Only God could forgive sins! It was blasphemy!

But it may be that Jesus never actually forgave anyone's sins, but was only telling them the simple truth: their sins were *already* forgiven. God does not hold anything against them. Nor ever would. God loves and accepts everyone, just as they are.

This was too radical a message to be received. The temple hierarchy decided he was too great a threat to their monopoly on religious authority. They could not suffer such a loose cannon blowing up their fragile collaboration with Rome. All their efforts to rein him in had failed; so they plotted to arrest him, and used the disillusionment of one of his own disciples to do it. Judas Iscariot, an outspoken zealot who had pinned his hopes on Jesus being the promised warrior messiah, agreed that Jesus was more of a danger than a help to Israel. The thirty pieces of silver were a ritual; his reasons for turning Jesus over to the authorities were largely altruistic—he truly believed it was what was best for the Jewish people.

Thus it was on the night of Passover that Judas led troops of the temple guard to a moonlit garden where, with a kiss, he delivered his rabbi over to his enemies. Jesus was tried and condemned for heresy. Unfortunately for the temple hierarchy, they did not have the authority to carry out the proscribed punishment: death. So they asked the Romans to do it for them. After much passing of the buck, the Romans agreed to do it, and along with two other criminals, Jesus was crucified on a hill outside Jerusalem.

Jesus hung on the cross for three hours before he expired and "gave up the ghost." The Christian scriptures say that when he died, the veil in the Jewish temple was rent in two, eliminating the barrier between humans and God; the dead rose from their graves; and the earth heaved in its grief. Jesus was laid in a borrowed tomb, which was sealed with the Roman governor's seal and guarded by Roman troops.

His followers were utterly lost in their grief. The women longed to anoint his body, as was the way of their people, but it was the Sabbath, and so they waited. Early on the first day of the week, however, the woman closest to Jesus' heart, Mary of Magdala, went out before the first light to tend to his body. When she arrived, she found the seal broken, the troops scattered, and the stone covering the mouth of the tomb rolled to the side. Her teacher's body was missing, and she panicked. She rushed out of the tomb, and was met by the gardener. As they spoke, she recognized him as Jesus himself, alive again and speaking to her.

She rushed to tell the others, who ran to the tomb to see for themselves. They did not know what to think, and thought perhaps Mary was hallucinating when she said she had seen their teacher alive. But later, Jesus himself came to them. The accounts vary: in some passages he seems to be a ghostly presence, incorporeal, able to walk through walls. But in others he has a solid body that the disciples can touch. After many such appearances, Jesus told his disciples to carry on his mission, bringing the good news of God's love and acceptance to people everywhere. Then he rose from their sight, and was gone.

His followers continued to stay together, and the Christian scriptures say that the spirit of God came upon them and gave them the same power to heal the sick and raise the dead, which it appeared that Jesus had (even though he very plainly said that it was not he who did it). They continued as a "school" within Judaism for many years, led by Jesus' brother, James, who was often in conflict with the religious leaders just as Jesus had been.

One of those who opposed Jesus' school was a zealous student of the law named Saul, who incited riots against these dangerous heretics who threatened the fate of Israel. Then, according to accounts recorded by Saul's followers, Saul was struck from his horse by a blinding vision. Jesus himself spoke to Saul, and reprimanded him for his persecutions. Saul became a believer in Jesus after that, changed his name to Paul, and began preaching to Jews and Gentiles alike outside of Israel.

There was much conflict between the earliest followers of Jesus (centered in Jerusalem and led by Jesus' own family) and the followers of Paul (who were mainly Gentiles in other regions of the Roman Empire). They had very different understandings of who Jesus was and what his mission was all about. Soon, other groups of Jesus followers sprung up, with even more wildly divergent notions.

The Jerusalem community led by James taught that Jesus was just an ordinary human, whom God had favored for his devotion to—and complete understanding of—the Jewish Law. They felt he was a new prophet who had come to complete Moses' mission, to proclaim God's unconditional forgiveness, and to end the temple sacrifices.

Gnostic Christians taught that Jesus was not human at all, but was a divine being who came from another, perfect, universe to wake humans up to the fact that they were imprisoned in a world of suffering, and that the Jewish God was only a misguided lesser deity, a pretender to the throne. Jesus only seemed to have a body, and on the cross he laughed at the silly humans who thought they were killing him. Other Christians would likewise say that Jesus was only divine, even if they did not deny the solidity of his body.

So who was Jesus, really? A man or a god? The Christians who followed Paul steered a middle course between these two options. Unlike the Gnostics, they affirmed the goodness of the Jewish God and the earth, but unlike the Jerusalem Christians, they believed that Jesus was a savior who had come down from heaven and taken a human form. The story of the virgin birth was popular in Paul's communities, and it helped to explain how Jesus could be both human and divine at the same time.

It was Paul's version of the Jesus story that really caught on. It spread like wildfire throughout the ancient world, exciting both Jews (for whom their messiah had finally come) and Gentiles (who were used to the notion that gods could have children who were both human and divine). But there continued to be much debate even within the ranks of Pauline Christianity: exactly how were Jesus and God related? In what way, exactly, was he divine, and just how human could he really be?

The debates raged for centuries. Some said that Jesus was just a man until his baptism, when Sophia, the Holy Wisdom of God by whose hand the world was made, entered into him (thus Jesus was a human man with a human soul, but was "possessed" by a holy spirit). Others said that Jesus was God himself, who took upon himself human flesh and lived among us. When he died on the cross, it was the Father himself who died, and rose himself from death.

At the council of Nicaea in 325 C.E., a middle course was once again maintained. It was decided that Jesus' life could have no meaning if he was not fully and completely human. If he had some divine edge, then his temptations would have meant nothing. But, it was also maintained, the divine work of salvation likewise could not be accomplished if Jesus was anything less than fully and completely God. The idea of the Trinity was made a doctrine, in spite of many references in the Christian scriptures that seemed to contradict it.

The leading theory of how Jesus saved human beings at that time is now known as the "recapitulation" theory. This holds that when Adam sinned, he dragged all of humanity with him into disobedience. Only a human life lived in perfect obedience to God's will could restore dignity to the human race, and break the power of death that held all in its thrall. Jesus lived this perfect life, the theory says, restored in us the image of God in which we were created, and broke the power of death to hold humans captive when he forged a path from the land of the dead so that all could follow him into eternal life.

Hand in hand with this theory, however, was the notion that God saves by subsumation. Jews are saved by joining themselves to the people of Israel—people are not saved as individuals, but by being subsumed into a group that will be saved by God. Paul re-visioned this idea by positing a parallel group for Gentiles: Christians are thus saved—again, not as individuals—but by joining themselves to the body of Christ, the "new Israel."

The church fathers taught that God cannot save what God does not assume. Since only a truly human soul could accomplish the task of recapitulation, Jesus must be wholly and completely human. But only God could accomplish the task of subsumation, so Jesus must also be fully and completely God. The apparent contradiction of how Jesus could be both fully God and fully human has confounded people ever since, especially Christians.

Eventually Christians began to see the universe in very mystical terms indeed. Eastern Orthodox Christians teach that, in Jesus, God made the first "joining" with creation, but through the work of the church, all people everywhere are being mystically joined with God. But it does not stop with humans: the work of mystical union once begun, divine rays from heaven penetrate the whole universe, and everything that is is being divinized, and subsumed into God. Jesus the carpenter from Nazareth had become the Cosmic Christ, making all things one, all things holy, all divine.

The Courage to Be Fully Human

In our work as spiritual guides, it is our work to notice how God is present in all things, how the Spirit is making all things holy, especially our directees. As part of the divinized universe, we can lay claim to the divinity that is our spiritual inheritance, while at the same time acknowledging that we cannot effectively do our work if we are not also fully and completely human. The balancing act that orthodox Christians insisted Jesus did is also present in our own ministry. The spirit of God is working in us and speaking through us, yet at the same time we are fallible, ephemeral, and human.

This seems like a conflict that is impossible to resolve, yet the example of Jesus shows us that this need not be so. In Jesus, God worked through those things which were imminently human—Jesus' passions, his ignorance, even his mistakes. When Jesus lost his temper and started driving people out of the temple with a whip, it was probably not his finest moment. Yet the Divine did not abandon him, it did not derail his ministry, nor did it invalidate his teachings of forgiveness and peace. Contradiction is part of the human condition, and the Divine used that which emerged from Jesus' humanness to accomplish the divine will just as much as that which emerged from his Godness. The Divine does the same through us.

For this to work, we must confront our egos, which want to take credit for everything we do. It is not our egos doing this work, but the Divine; we are not in control of the process, we only witness it and encourage it. Jesus did not, in orthodox teaching, raise himself from the dead, but was raised by the power of God. Likewise, we do not raise our clients to higher states of spiritual awareness. The Divine raises them, we are simply fortunate enough, like Mary, to behold the emergence of the new beings our clients are becoming.

Because it is not us actually doing the work, because we cannot take credit for it, we must be very careful not to overesteem our role. When clients come to us, there is the tendency on the part of many of them to view us as spiritually superior to themselves in some way. It is not unusual, I have found, when a new client enters my office, to discover that he or she has me on some kind of pedestal.

I won't deny how good this feels—it's a thrill to be so esteemed and looked-up-to, to bask in the starry-eyed adoration of a new client. And if what we are about here is shoring up our own fragile self-images, that would be lovely. But such adulation is disastrous for the spiritual direction relationship. As long as I am on a pedestal, I am no good to my clients. The wise and perfected being they perceive me to be cannot help but disappoint them, which can severely damage the spiritual guidance relationship. It is best to climb down from the pedestal early in the game.

Such projections are inevitable in our culture, unfortunately. We are socialized to see the world in dualistic terms—this is especially true of spiritual realities. It is partly due to the influence of Gnostic Christianity that we tend to value spirit over matter, heaven over earth, men over women, etc. Because of this dualistic orientation, we often view ourselves as spiritually lowly, and idealize spiritual leaders as being somehow holier than we are, better than we are—even, in some cases, perfect.

The Christian tradition sees any false god we might set up as an idol, and idols must be smashed to free us from their power. The outrageous esteem in which we hold some spiritual leaders is just such an idol, and we must be careful not to let ourselves be idolized. No true ministry can occur when we assume a mantle of spiritual mastery, because then we reinforce the hierarchical view our clients—quite naturally, yet mistakenly—enter the session with.

This does two disastrous things: it denies our clients access to Divinity (they cannot truly advance due to the unspoken fear—on their part or ours—that they may surpass us and threaten our perceived superiority) and we deny ourselves humanity (which we desperately need access to in session, because, face it, we screw up all the time, and need to be able to say so).

To be effective spiritual guides we must eschew false dualities, even if it means an initial disappointment for our clients. They must see right up front that we are not gods, but fellow, fallible humans. We are not advanced sages going ahead to straighten their way, we are fellow travelers who are just as vulnerable, fallible, and susceptible to self-deception as they. The *Tao Te Ching* asks us directly, "Being both body and spirit, can you embrace unity and not be fragmented?" Can you, in your practice of spiritual guidance, fully embrace your humanness, get your ego out of the way, and allow the Divine within you to do its true work?

In Paul's letter to the Philippians, he wrote, "Have this attitude in yourselves which was also in Christ Jesus, who, although he existed in the form of God, did not regard equality with God a thing to be grasped, but emptied himself, taking the form of a bond-servant, and being made in the likeness of humans."[23] Just as Jesus, in Paul's view, descended from heaven and took his place alongside his fellow humans; so we also must climb down from our pedestals and join our clients as equals and partners, not as experts who alone know the path, but as fellow adventurers expecting to be surprised.

If we cannot agree to this, or if we forget our humanness and begin to believe our own PR, then we become a danger to our clients and we should cease our work immediately. Once we begin to show a false face to our clients; we lie to them, to ourselves, and to the Divine. What is more, we begin to hide or repress those parts of ourselves that do not fit the image being projected onto us (or that we ourselves are projecting). This becomes shadow material—which Jungian psychology identifies as any rejected parts of ourselves. Any part that is denied expression will leap out in neurotic or inappropriate ways, and will inevitably do harm to our clients.

The alternative is to simply embrace ourselves as the Divine does, with all our warts, shadows, and all the icky parts we would rather people not know about. Just as the early church fathers said, "God cannot save what God does not assume," so we cannot redeem those parts of ourselves that we reject.

In the recently discovered Gospel of Thomas, Jesus is reported as having said, "If you bring forth those things that are within you, that which you bring forth will save you. If you fail to bring forth that which is within you, what you fail to bring forth will condemn you." In order to be whole people, to do our work with integrity and honesty, we must show up with our whole selves, even those parts we do not like. If we can, we will discover something frightening and profound—that it is those very parts we reject that make us good spiritual guides.

The Power of Vulnerability

When I begin supervising a new spiritual guide, the panicked phone call comes in like clockwork. I got just such a call from Karen. She had an initial meeting with her first client the next day, and was a little hysterical. "Wait, I can't see a client, I don't know what I'm doing!" she shrieked.

"You're right," I told her. "You don't know what you are doing. And the moment you have a sense that you *do* know what you are doing, you should quit."

"But what if I make a mistake?"

"Let me put your mind at ease," I said. "You will make *lots* of mistakes. Get used to it. I make them all the time. It's one of the things I'm best at."

"You're no help at all!" She complained, "I don't think I can *do* this!"

"Trust that feeling!" I said, "Because you *can't* do this. None of us can. So get out of the way and let the Divine do it."

"I'm scared!"

"I'd be worried if you weren't," I told her. "So long as you are scared, you're trustworthy."

Okay, in print this doesn't look very comforting, but with a little cajoling good humor, this confounding Zen-master approach did put Karen at ease—a little.

Doing spiritual guidance is an exercise in humility. First, we must empty ourselves of the notion that we know what we are doing. We do our best work when we do not have an agenda. Once we feel we have our clients all figured out and know exactly what is "wrong" with them and how to fix it, or how to "get them" from point A to point B, then we might as well hang it up and go into some other business, because we are not going to be any help to the Divine—or our clients. The truth is every client is an unquantifiable mystery—known only to the Divine, and to a lesser degree, to themselves.

Entering a session with no idea what we are about requires a great deal of trust, but this kind of trust in the Divine is precisely our stock-in-trade as spiritual guides. If we can enter each session utterly clueless we will be far ahead of those who think they know exactly what they are doing, and will serve our clients much better.

For truly, we are *not* competent to do this work. None of us has the transcendent perspective needed to understand how all things will work together for our clients' formation. None of us possesses the degree of omniscience required for such responsibility. Fortunately for us, we do not have to. We must have the humility of spirit to get out of the way—to empty our own boats, as Chuang-Tzu said in chapter two—so that the Divine, which is alone qualified to do this work, can get down to business.

As Alan Watts once wrote, there is wisdom in insecurity. Most of the abuse that has occurred in the history of spiritual guidance has happened because of guides who were sure they knew what the Divine required, wanted, demanded of their clients. We can avoid this danger by cherishing our incompetence, our ignorance, our ineptitude. If we can embrace these parts of ourselves, then we make room for the Divine to do what most needs be done. Nobody puts the incompetent, the ignorant, or the inept on pedestals, so if we can cling to these qualities, we will be safe, and safely grounded.

When we give ourselves permission to simply be who we are, we enter the session expecting to be surprised, to learn, to be changed even as our clients are changed. If we feel at liberty to be human, we can say, "I don't know" when we are uncertain. We can cry when we are touched, we can ask for a moment if we are having feelings we need to sort out, or can excuse ourselves if we need a drink of water or to go to the restroom. We are empowered to say, "I'm sorry" when we are wrong, ask forgiveness when we have overstepped our bounds or have hurt a clients' feelings, or can share an anectdote in which we come off looking less than stellar.

Just as Jesus, in Christian teaching, left behind his glory, took the form of a mewling infant, and entered the harsh world of flesh and blood in the most vulnerable of conditions, we, too, are being called to leave our certainty, our security, and, indeed, our power outside the spiritual guidance room. If we can do this, we will experience an amazing freedom, one that has a profound effect in the spiritual guidance session. In being human, we give our clients permission to do the same. And instead of simply setting ourselves up to fall from our perches high on our pedestals (and perpetuating a problematic dualism along the way), we model a divinized humanity that can love and be loved in all its messy and vulnerable glory.

For our own problems, struggles, mistakes, and yes, even sins, can, if we are aware of them, give us the gift of empathy for the trials our clients face. This allows us to respond to them from a place of compassion rather than judgment or impatience.

What is uncanny is that the issues your clients will bring to session are invariably your own. The very things you struggle with will come up again and again in your own clients. It is a strange and inexplicable universal law. I often have the bizarre and disembodied experience of listening to my mouth tell clients the very things I most need to hear. Of course, discernment is called for to make sure that it is Providence at play here, rather than simply projection. But very often, in my experience, the trickster Divine is getting two for one, if you are wise enough to listen to the advice coming through you.

One spiritual guide I was supervising complained loudly, "How can I help her [my client] when I'm so hopeless about it [a specific issue] myself?"

"By not pretending to have it figured out," I told him. "After all, you don't know where your client is heading. Perhaps, wherever it is the Divine is leading, you are going there together." The marvelous thing about being a wounded healer is that in helping others to heal, you will invariably find healing for yourself.

The Willingness to Be Sacrificed

As early as the middle of the first century, Christians began to interpret Jesus' life through the lens of Jewish scripture. Many passages that had seemed obscure suddenly made sense in light of Jesus' story. One passage that leaped out at the early Pauline Christians was a verse in Isaiah, "with his stripes we are healed" (53:5, KJV). Christians interpreted this to mean that Jesus' crucifixion was somehow redemptive, that his suffering was offered in exchange for ours. Because he had been wounded, we can be healed.

This teaching took nearly a thousand years to reach the form that most Christians are familiar with today, but the basic notion has been around a long time. This is the idea of the scapegoat, where one being bears the burden of sickness or sin for another.

Unfortunately, Christians in the West went a little overboard with this notion, and emphasized Jesus' suffering to the exclusion of any other portion of his ministry—Eastern Christians do not share this obsession, and view the resurrection as the salvific focus of the faith. But in the West, his crucifixion alone was seen as salvific, creating a cult of suffering we are still wrestling with. For in the understandable impulse to be like Jesus, this meant, for Westerners, sacrificing ourselves even as he did, glorifying suffering, and even, in some cases, making it compulsory.

This has been particularly tragic for women, who, while being encouraged to sacrifice their own hopes, dreams, and health for their loved ones, even as men were, were not compensated on the other hand with any of the privileges of power or authority held by men. Their lot has been only to sacrifice—their reward would be in the hereafter. The poor of both sexes have known similar suffering, and neither had much power to object.

Yet, even though it has been sorely abused, the intuition that suffering is somehow redemptive is not completely without foundation. The willingness to delay gratification for a greater good, or to tolerate some hardship for the sake of another is the mark of basic maturity. But "willingness" is the operative word. Suffering cannot be redemptive if it is enforced, or even psychologically coerced. The willing suffering of Jesus is echoed in every parent who has gone without food so that a child could eat, in every soldier who threw himself into harm's way to save his comrades or homeland. And these are true gifts, indeed. We will frequently be given the opportunity, in our ministry as spiritual guides, to offer such gifts to our clients, but they must not be given grudgingly. If they are to do any good, they must be given with love, and without reservation, even at some personal cost.

People have projected all kinds of things onto Jesus: the zealots were sure he was a military leader, the temple authorities were sure he was a heretic, the Gnostics were certain he was an emissary from an alien god, and so on. Every religious group has fashioned Jesus in its own image, and put its own words in his mouth. Everyone has projected a different image onto him, and he has borne them all in silence, even unto death. Jesus bears the collective projections of innumerable peoples, and continues to do so to this very day.

In our practice as spiritual guides, people likewise project onto us, some of it accurate, some of it ludicrous. The question is, can we bear the weight of these projections? And are we able to do so willingly, even when they are painful?

As a spiritual authority figure you will without a doubt receive punishment from people lashing out at you from their religious wounding. And since there is no shortage of religious wounding, it is likely that you will encounter much of this in your practice.

When a young Jewish man named Stan began work with Carl, a Lutheran pastor and interfaith spiritual guide, all seemed pretty normal on the surface. But about six months into their work, new thread began to emerge. Stan had started to research his family history, and had asked his grandparents to tell him about their own folks. Since their parents had died in the concentration camps, this opened a floodgate of memories and anger. Stan listened for hours in horrified amazement. Their own rage and grief became his, and he had many nightmares about his great-grandparents. Though he did not intend to, Stan brought a lot of his anger into his sessions with Carl. Since it was Germans—Lutherans!—who were responsible for the unspeakable evil toward Stan's great-grandparents, he lashed out.

Carl came from a line of Scandinavian Lutherans, but he knew this did not matter to Stan. Carl knew that he was not himself responsible for the suffering of Stan's relatives, and he was tempted to object, to walk out, or to end the session. But instead of defending himself or derailing the process, he was able to muster sufficient internal distance to remain present throughout the session. Eventually Stan finished venting his rage, and wept.

Carl reached out and touched his shoulder gently. When Stan looked up he saw that Carl had been crying, too. "Stan, I'm so, so sorry for what happened to your great-grandparents. They suffered a horrible, unspeakable evil, and you have every right to feel the things you are feeling. As a Lutheran, and as a Christian, I am deeply ashamed of what my own people have done to yours. I am so sorry."

Carl did not need to cop to something that was not his, and yet his ability to bear Stan's projections resulted in an opportunity for empathic connection, for healing that might not otherwise have occurred.

As spiritual guides, we are, in a way, symbolic of every religious authority in existence. And any anger held by the client will consciously or unconsciously be revealed given enough time. Every group has its own sins to account for. If you are a Christian, for instance, you may apologize on behalf of the church, as Carl did, for surely there is much in Christian history to atone for.

The sins of the past will not be the only ones hurled at us in session, however. Carl was not responsible for Stan's anger, yet there are many times when feelings emerge in a session that we may indeed feel some responsibility for. Every variety of wounding is likely to impinge on the spiritual guidance session. If we can be true to what is within us, acknowledging both our light and shadow, then we can cop to most things thrown at us.

If a client attacks you by saying, "You're so judgmental!" you have a couple of options. You could throw down a boundary—"Hey, you're talking about your parents, not me!" This might be true, and it might even be an appropriate response if the client is triggering a wound in you that is too big for you to contain in the session.

Yet it is probably true of most of us that, on some level, we *are* judgmental. If we can cop to this, the level of empathy and trust in the spiritual guidance relationship will not be breached, but strengthened and deepened. To be able to present a human and fallible human face to a client is a great gift, and models a spiritual maturity that your client may not witness very often. If we can bear these projections, even though it may be painful in the moment, our clients may find the grace to work through their accusations and heal them, or even own them for themselves.

Can you allow your client to vent all of his anger at organized religion at you? This will probably depend on the level of your own woundedness, the number of accusations you are willing to cop to (whether as an individual or as a community representative), and your willingness and ability to sit with uncomfortable feelings.

I recognize that this is edging dangerously close to the use of transference in psychotherapy, and I am not suggesting that we foster transference or work with it consciously very far beyond the simple ability to endure uncomfortable projections. But to think that we can possibly do our work without encountering the projections of our clients is nothing short of fantasy. The question is, when such projections emerge, what is your capacity to carry them?

We can carry more than projections, however, and this finds us firmly on our home territory of spiritual guidance. In the writings of the desert fathers and mothers there is a story of a brother who had committed a grievous sin. He went to Abba Lot, and was very nervous, pacing about, unable to sit. Abba Lot said, "What is the matter, brother?"

He said, "I have committed a great fault and cannot acknowledge it to the priests."

The old man said, "Confess it to me, and I will carry it."

The brother swallowed hard and said, "Okay, but it's a bad one."

"I am ready."

"I made sacrifices at the pagan temple and bought time with the sacred prostitutes there as well."

The old man pursed his lips and rocked back and forth for a while.

"This is not so bad," he said. "Don't be too hard on yourself. Go back to your cave, fast for a couple of days, and I will carry the blame for half of your transgression."[24]

Though it may seem strange to our postmodern sensibilities, the desert fathers and mothers modeled for us a practice of metaphysical exchange that is just as effective today as it was in the third century C.E. Just as some Christians believe Jesus took upon himself the sins of others, we can, in fact, carry the psychological and moral burdens of our clients, if they will allow us to do so.

Not too long ago I had a client who was very anxious indeed about a visit to some relatives who had been very unkind to her. Religious fundamentalists, they mocked her eclectic spiritual path, and she was becoming more and more upset as her travel date approached. I told her, "I know you are feeling a lot of fear right now, and it seems you don't know what to do with it." She nodded. "If you like," I told her, "I will carry half of your fear so that the burden will be less for you."

Her eyes widened. "Can you do that?"

"I can, but only if you are willing to let half of it go."

We held hands and she breathed onto my hands. I let go and moved my hands to my breast. "I'll carry this." I smiled at her, and she breathed deeply. I could see her physically relax, and later she told me that the exchange had helped her immensely.

Though we typically want to reject the seemingly miraculous in our culture, the effectiveness of this practice cannot be denied, and I am left with the conclusion that it is simply the result of some cosmic law operative in the universe. The theology of exchange was developed by Charles Williams in the mid-twentieth century, and it is a very useful tool to have at the ready. If we are willing, and if our clients are willing, we can indeed carry for them anxiety, guilt, sin—or even physical pain.

An apocryphal story told about C.S. Lewis relates that when his wife, Joy, was dying of cancer, she was unable to rest due to the pain. He invited her to allow the pain to enter into him—she consented, and he bore her pain for an hour while she slept deeply for the first time in days.

While they may be initially incredulous, the practice of exchange can bring great relief to our clients. But it comes at a cost, for we must endure some discomfort ourselves if we are willing to truly bear their burdens. The consolation in this, however, is that such burdens are not nearly as heavy for us as they are for our clients, because the burdens are not ours. There is a grace that comes with such willing sacrifice that makes these burdens easy. Jesus said, "Come to me, all ye that labor and are heavy laden, and I will give you rest. . . . For my yoke is easy, and my burden is light" (Matt 11:28, 30, KJV). All burdens are light when they are not our own. Like Jesus, we can take some of the weight off of those we serve.

Christians the world over see themselves as the "body of Christ." This is both a figurative and a literal image. In one sense individuals feel they have been joined to Christ's body in the same way that Jews have been joined to Israel. But in a more literal sense, many Christians understand themselves to be the ongoing presence of Jesus in the world. Thérèse of Lisieux once wrote, "Jesus has no hands on earth but mine." Jesus did so much good during his ministry: he befriended the friendless, and gave dignity and hope back to his society's outcasts. He had the courage to be vulnerable, and bore the projections of those around him, even at great personal cost.

As spiritual guides, we will often be called upon to do the same. The Divine has no hands on earth but ours, we are the ones who have been called, and we have chosen to do the hard work of redemption on behalf of our clients. We will not do it effectively in spite of our fallibility, vulnerability, and humanity, but rather because of it. This is the path of the wounded healer, and if we wish to be any help to our clients at all, we have no choice but to walk it.

8

Islam and Spiritual Discipline

In the early seventh century a young man, deeply disturbed by the troubles facing his community, climbed Mount Hira to pray. He entered a cave near the mountain's peak, and as he did every year at this time, poured out his heart before al-Lah, "the God." The silence of the cave soothed his spirit, and though he was filled with turmoil, he rested a bit easier here.

And then one night, as he was sleeping after a long day of prayer, a presence seized him. He felt like his ribs were being crushed, and an angel spoke to him strange and beautiful words that were both frightening and prophetic. He was shaken by this experience, and when he returned to his city, he told only his wife and her cousin about what had happened.

"Maybe these words are from God," they told him, but he was not sure. The visitations continued, each one as painful and frightening as the last. And more words came, too. Gradually he understood that al-Lah was speaking to him and through him; these words were not simply the result of a dream or an overactive imagination, but were words of a new scripture, a gift from the God.

Muhammad believed that Allah had sent prophets to all of the peoples around them, and delivered to every people a holy book. But God had sent no one to the Arab peoples. Did God not care about them? The Zoroastrians had Zarathushtra, and through him the holy Gathas, the Jews had been sent Moses, and the Torah was their holy book. Allah had sent Jesus to the

Christians, and the Gospels were for them words of life. But where was the prophet for the Arabs, and where was their holy book?

The young man, Muhammad of the Quraysh tribe, felt a mixture of gratitude and fear. He was grateful that al-Lah had not forsaken them, but he was terrified to have been the one chosen to deliver the new holy book.

He had every right to be scared. His people were not likely to be receptive to the kind of messages he was receiving. His was a deeply divided society, composed of many tribes which all seemed to be at one another's throats. Blood feuds were rampant, and the antagonism that kept them at odds with each other prevented them from building the kind of prosperous societies that their neighbors enjoyed. Furthermore, the tribes all honored their own gods, and were looked down upon by their Jewish and Christian neighbors as being pagans, culturally backward and religiously unsophisticated.

But the revelations Muhammad was receiving were calling for a new kind of society to come into being. It prophesied a society that honored one God, who upheld justice for the weak and the vulnerable, and who outlawed revenge and bloodshed. The revelations called for the birth of the Just Community (*ummah*), united by one faith and governed by one law. A way out of the wilderness of tribal warfare, conflicting traditions, and rampant greed was being made known to Muhammad, but he was terrified to speak it. Surely he would be killed, for his revelations called for an end to the only political and cultural system his people had ever known, and those in power would not relinquish it without a fight.

At first Muhammad just kept quiet, sharing his revelations only with his family, but after a couple of years, he felt moved to begin preaching. Some believed him, and followed his teachings. But most ridiculed, or simply ignored him. But slowly Muhammad made headway. One man, named Umar ibn al-Khattab, fiercely denounced Muhammad and his message. A firm believer in the old gods, Umar was also quite a devotee of Arabic poetry. He had spoken against those teachings he had heard about second hand, but when he actually heard the words of the revelation with his own ears, the beauty of the poetry utterly undid him, and his heart melted. He became a believer in the new religion, and many others followed suit.

It didn't help that the revelation directly opposed much in Arabian society. The Arabs were a proud people, and unlike those in the empires that surrounded them, they served no monarch, and bowed to no man.

Muhammad knew that it was precisely this fierce pride that was the cause of so much suffering among his people. It was pride that prevented one tribe from forgiving another, allowing the rivalries to escalate and wreak such havoc on society. Pride caused men to oppress even the women in their own families; and where tribal law insisted that the poor and weak be provided for, the booming trade business, which had arisen in just the last generation, had brought with it a pervasive greed that ignored the tribal wisdom.

In contrast to this, Muhammad's revelation insisted that all people, from high to low, humble themselves and bow—not before any human being, but before God; and not just in their hearts, but in their bodies; and not just in private, but in public. The new religion became known as "Islam," which means "submission." Muhammad insisted that believers bow down before Allah publicly not just once, but several times every day.

It was a program of aggressive reeducation. Instead of fighting one another, Muhammad insisted that the greatest struggle—or *jihad*—was an internal one. It was a struggle against pride and the ego, greed and selfishness, cruelty and stubbornness. It insisted that the good of society as a whole outweighed the good of one's own family or tribe, and that forming the Just Community was more important than accumulating personal wealth or defending the honor of one's own clan.

It was a hard message to hear, and fierce opposition to the prophet's message arose. After about four years of preaching, nearly seventy families had converted to Islam, but the chiefs of the tribes had become openly hostile. They forbade any of their peoples to trade with Muhammad's tribe or any of his converts, or even to marry anyone in his tribe. Later, Muhammad's uncle died, and without a powerful clan member to protect him, he became easy prey for those who opposed him.

Then an unexpected thing happened. An envoy from another city, Yathrib, sought Muhammad out and made him a proposition. Their own community was as torn apart by tribal feuding as his own, but they had had much contact with Jews and were not unfamiliar with monotheistic faith. They offered to convert to Islam if Muhammad would move to their city and rule them, end their infighting and factionalism, and bring the dream of the Just Community to fruition in their midst. It seemed too good to be true, but soon Muhammad was convinced of their sincerity, and under the cover of night, the Muslims of Mecca slipped out of the city and made their way to Yathrib.

They renamed their city al-Medina, "the city," and set about creating the Just Community as directed by Muhammad's continuing visions. They built a mosque, devoted themselves to daily prayer and other spiritual disciplines, and forged alliances with the local tribes.

Part of the appeal of Islam was that Muhammad insisted that it was not a new religion. It was the proclamation to the Arab peoples of the same truth revealed to other peoples by various prophets throughout the ages, among them Abraham, Moses, David, Zarathushtra, and Jesus. Instead of rejecting these previous prophets, Mohammad's revelations affirmed their validity, and invited the Arab peoples to share in the communion with the one God that Jews, Christians, and Zoroastrians enjoyed. They were being given an opportunity to leave their petty factionalisms behind, and to gain the sophistication and respect that the other monotheistic faiths possessed.

Far from insisting that everyone convert to Islam, therefore, Muhammad affirmed the validity of the faith of the Jews and Christians in their midst. In ruling Medina he achieved something that no one had ever seen before: in the service of the Just Community, the people there put aside their tribal allegiances and religious rivalries. Instead, each of the local tribes offered their allegiance, and their swords, to Muhammad, and by thus banding together they not only defended themselves against attacks from outsiders, but maintained a peace among themselves that was previously unheard of.

For those back in Mecca, this was perceived to be heresy. How dare Muhammad value Jews, Christians, and other tribes above those of his own blood? They mounted a military campaign against the Muslims at Medina in 625, and almost destroyed the Just Community. Muhammad regrouped, however, and at the Battle of the Trench, the Muslims employed guerrilla tactics that utterly threw the Meccans. Outnumbered three to one, Muhammad had stolen victory from under the noses of his enemies.

Not all of Muhammad's enemies were outside his gates, however. Pagan families residing in Medina, unhappy with the Islamic law enforced by the prophet, plotted against him, as did several powerful Jewish families. Muhammad tried to make peace with them, but in the end, force was necessary to safeguard the fragile community at Medina. This shook Muhammad to the core, and with great sadness he laid down his sword and declared that he would make peace with the Meccans. He decided to take the sacred pilgrimage, the *hajj*, and asked for volunteers to join him.

This was, in some people's eyes, a very foolhardy thing to do. Pilgrims are forbidden to carry weapons, and Muhammad and anyone who went with them would be walking unprotected right into their enemies' hands. Nevertheless, over 1,000 pilgrims joined him. He knew he would be safe if he could just get within the city walls, where religious custom protected all pilgrims. The Meccans knew he was coming, however, and tried to prevent his entry.

But Muhammad was as skilled at making friends as he was enemies. Many of the nomadic Bedouin tribes in the area were impressed by Muhammad's leadership, and some of them had even converted to Islam. Some of those who had not converted nevertheless entered into treaties with him and put their own swords at his disposal. Because of the friendship of these nomads, Muhammad escaped capture, and achieved the sanctuary of the city walls.

Impressed by this adventure, even more Bedouins flocked to Muhammad's cause, and a couple of years later, when the Meccans violated the fragile trust established with the Medina community, Muhammad marched on his former home with 10,000 troops. The Meccans, realizing they had no chance against such a force, opened the gates and accepted their exiled son as their prophet and ruler.

Two years later, Muhammad died. By that time almost all of the tribes, which had formerly been at each other's throats, had put their tribal traditions aside and embraced Islam, trading the endless cycle of bloodshed and revenge for the dream of the Just Community.

Disputes about who should lead after the death of the prophet split the community. Most thought that the person in the community best qualified to be a leader should assume control—in the early days, this meant one of Muhammad's closest advisors. This created the *caliphate* leading the largest branch of Islam, the Sunnis. But some thought that Muhammad's closest male relative should lead, a young man named Ali. Those who followed him became known as the Shi'a.

Five Pillars of Islam

Though Muslims continue to disagree about which lineage is the legitimate one, all Muslims agree on the essentials of the faith: the prophethood of Muhammad and the necessity of the individual's submission to Allah. The pride that prevented the early tribal leaders from cooperating was not unique to them—it is a universal condition that all Muslims must confront; indeed all people of faith deal with this in their own way.

How do I insure that my concern for others outweighs my concern for my own personal gain? How do I temper my own self-involvement so that I am aware of the needs of others in my family and community? How do I get my ego out of the way so that the Divine can truly shine through me? These are prime questions not only for people of faith everywhere, but for the practice of spiritual guidance as well.

Muhammad devised five "pillars" upon which the faith would rest. These "spiritual supports" are actually spiritual disciplines designed to ensure that believers put the community before their own gain. These five are 1) the profession of faith; 2) prayer; 3) almsgiving; 4) fasting; and 5) pilgrimage.

We in the West have become allergic to language that smacks of "discipline." This is partly due to the fact, I think, that some of us were raised in rigid religious traditions, which demanded disciplines from us often seeming unconnected to real life, not serving to connect us to the Divine, and feeling more like punishments than helpful practices. The rest of us were raised in a culture informed by such traditions. This is unfortunate, as no spiritual discipline can be of any use when it is coerced.

Recently my nephew complained to my mother, "Why do I have to fast?" "Who told you to fast?" she asked. "My Dad," he answered. My mother was in the tricky position of answering a theological question honestly while at the same time not contradicting her son-in-law. "Sometimes it helps us pray when we fast—the rumbling in our tummies reminds us to bring our prayer before God again and again throughout the day. But it has to be something you choose to do or God doesn't want you to do it. No one can make you fast."

No spiritual practice can help us if we don't want to do it. It only results in a show of religion, and, inevitably, resentment. But if we are serious about growing spiritually we will find ourselves willing to make some sacrifices to help speed us along our path. A spiritual discipline, willingly undertaken, can ground us, strengthen our spiritual resolve, teach us, and yes, help us overcome that pesky ego.

As spiritual guides, it is helpful to have a good assortment of spiritual disciplines in our "toolbox." Understanding the history, purpose, and a variety of methods for each discipline will help us know when to recommend a spiritual practice to our clients, and which disciplines might be appropriate. Let's look first at the five "Pillars of Islam," and then a few disciplines from other traditions that will be helpful to have at our disposal.

The Profession of Faith. Though many religions have long and compli-cated processes for conversion, becoming a Muslim is very easy indeed. All one must do is confess publicly, and with sincerity, "I bear witness that there is no god but Allah and that Muhammad is his prophet." At that point one is accepted into the Muslim community, with no questions asked. A practicing Muslim will repeat this profession daily.

Some sort of profession of faith is important for many religions, and it may in fact be important for our clients, as well. When clients first begin spiritual guidance, we often will ask them to tell us their spiritual histories. It is in the process of telling our story to someone else that we discover what is really true for us. And since our spirituality cannot help but to develop and change, the story will most likely change each time it is told, if only subtly.

When Brian first came to see Becky, he told her about his recent baptism into the Baptist faith. Since giving one's "testimony" is an important part of this tradition, he recounted with pride his testimony as he had just given it recently at church. Becky, a Roman Catholic, had felt a little uncomfortable with such a straightforward, unabashed statement of his commitment, since such personal declarations are not part of her own tradition. But she stayed with it, and after that first week, the sessions seemed more like what Becky was used to.

Then, after a couple of years, it was clear that something was shifting for Brian. A friend had introduced him to the *Tao Te Ching*, and he was clearly shaken by the wisdom he encountered there. It contradicted his notion that only the Christian tradition contained any real truth, and led him to explore other faith traditions as well. He read widely in world religions, and even be-gan to incorporate meditation into his prayer life. Although it was scary at first, Becky encouraged Brian to stay with the feelings and thoughts that were emerging from his studies, and helped him to pray through each one of them.

About three years after they started meeting together, Becky asked Brian to give his testimony again. He froze in horror at first, wondering how to fit everything he had encountered in the past year into the traditional form he was familiar with. But then he smiled, relaxed, and began, "When I first came to know Jesus, he liberated me. And he keeps on liberating me, too, from every box I try to build." A few weeks later, Brian stood up in church and gave his testimony in public once again. As his church was in the liberal

American Baptist tradition, his testimony was embraced. Indeed, he later told Becky, there was not a dry eye in the house.

It is important to tell our story many times, if only to help us to be conscious of how we have grown and what our faith looks like to us *now*. Saying what we believe is a revelatory act, for the hearer as well as the speaker. Professing one's faith is not only a statement of personal truth, but it also implies a commitment to the path we are on.

Daily Prayer. Muslim tradition requires a faithful believer to pray five times each day: at dawn, noon, midafternoon, sunset, and evening. These prayers are performed using a ritual called "bowing," in which the person praying stands, bows, kneels, and prostrates him or herself while reciting the proscribed prayers. All prayer is done facing Mecca, and most prayers are repeated several times.

Often, Muslims will carry a prayer rug with them so that they can properly perform this discipline wherever they happen to be. All prayers can be done in groups or individually, with the exception of the Friday noon prayer, which Muslim men must perform at a mosque in community with other Muslims. (Muslim women may join the men for Friday prayers, but are not required to do so.) In cities where there is a sizable Muslim population, a muezzin will give the call to prayer from the mosque to alert observant Muslims to the proper times for prayer.

Such a regular discipline of prayer accomplishes a number of things. First, it helps the believer to keep his or her priorities straight. If all of life simply stops five times a day in deference to the Divine, it is fairly clear what is most important in life. One's work is not more important than the Divine, nor is one's family. Everything must simply be dropped until one's obligation is fulfilled. This also helps keep the ego in check. To prostrate one's self is a humbling activity, but to do so several times per day is a way to retrain the mind, keep the ego in its proper place, and to orient one's life to the spiritual rather than the material.

All of these, however, are psychological benefits. True spiritual benefits result as well, as the soul is trained to turn to the Divine in times of prosperity and famine, of both peace and trouble. When in the course of one's day, whether met by good news or bad, one's first impulse is to give it over to the Divine, intimacy and true reliance upon divinity is fostered, encouraged, and strengthened.

The Jewish tradition also does this well with its emphasis on blessings. An observant Jew may bless God for everything he or she encounters. There is a blessing to be said for almost every daily activity, even for turning on a light switch. While at first that might seem to the casual observer a little obsessive, consider the benefits: even the most mundane of activities is divinized and oriented to the Holy. The division between sacred and secular disintegrates, until one is only living in one world—the spiritual one.

Most faith traditions honor some sort of prayer, whether it is formal or informal, individual or corporate, silent or spoken. All prayer serves to orient one's life toward the Divine, to remind one of one's role in the great scheme of things (whatever one perceives that to be), and to help one find the proper balance between pride and humility.

There are many forms of prayer, each of them beneficial in their own ways to the spiritual life. Just as any real communication requires both speaking and listening, prayer is no different. If prayer is speaking, meditation is listening, and both are important for a well-rounded prayer life.

Active forms of prayer—in which people speak or perform rituals— include petition (where we ask the Divine to help us or someone else), praise and thanksgiving, singing, liturgy, affirmations, and even confrontation (where we confront the Divine when we feel let down or even betrayed). For Sufis—Islamic mystics—dancing is a form of active prayer (or, more accurately, whirling in an ecstatic state).

Passive forms of prayer—in which people contemplate or listen for the voice of the Divine—include meditation, zazen, contemplation, and just *being* in the presence of the Holy.

Some forms of prayer such as *lectio divina* (holy reading) incorporate both active and passive forms into a single practice. Labyrinth walking and doing artwork are also forms of prayer that combine active and passive modes. Spiritual discernment, which we talked about at length a couple of chapters ago, is also an activity that requires both active and passive methods.

While those who follow theistic traditions tend more toward active prayer, those who do not have a theistic conception of divinity (such as Buddhists) lean more toward passive modes of prayer. Spiritual guides must be sensitive to such tendencies in different traditions, and yet still be ready to suggest less-familiar practices when it seems helpful to do so.

For those with no conception of divinity, such as agnostics or atheists, both active and passive forms are likewise important. Active forms might include public service (such as volunteering at a soup kitchen, protesting injustice, or being a big brother or sister), while passive forms might include insight meditation (where one clears the mind and waits to see what images or ideas emerge). Such practices can lead one to a more conscious, balanced, and meaningful life, even if it does not include conscious communion with the Divine.

A great deal of time in spiritual guidance is often devoted to discussing a client's prayer life. Sometimes a person will come to spiritual guidance precisely because his or her prayer life no longer gives him or her the satisfaction that it used to, or because his or her prayer seems to be changing, reorienting toward some unknown goal or object, which the client needs help to discern.

Spiritual guides can help their clients by employing both active and passive forms within each session, as well. It is always a good idea to pray for one's client before a session begins, as well as to pray for one's self to be a good listener who will have the proper words at the ready just when they are needed. Likewise, a guide must always be open to the prompting of the Divine. One of my students says that she tries to "speak only when spoken through." To do this, one must be a good listener, being not only attentive to the client, but to the Divine as well.

This can sometimes be very scary. Very often, I will be sitting with a client, and a thought will nudge at my brain forcefully. Now, I haven't much time for discernment at such times, and frequently, I will internally protest these thoughts. "I can't say that!" I say, to myself, or to the Divine, or perhaps to my own conscience. "That's too directive," or, "That's inappropriate," or sometimes even, "That's malpractice!" Like Muhammad, sometimes the messages that come through me frighten me, and I am afraid to speak them. Sometimes my internal protestations are correct, and I discern that the right thing to do is keep my mouth shut, and nod as if nothing was happening other than damn good listening. At other times, however, the thought nudging at my brain is more like a battering ram, and demands to be spoken. My brain will be saying, "No, no, no . . ." and, as if watching my body from above, I see my mouth opening and hear the forbidden words come out. Then I tense and wait for the backlash—which almost never comes.

Usually, when a thought so forcefully suggests itself, it is one of those instances of being "spoken through," and as scary as it is, the best thing to do is simply cooperate and hang on for the ride. Of course, on occasion, a client will also think one of these thoughts—which become statements—is inappropriate and take umbrage. This does not mean it was the wrong thing to say, however, and after the client cools down he or she will often see the wisdom in such words.

Because these sorts of discernments must be made quickly, and because this sort of thing happens in almost every session, it is important for the spiritual guide to be "spiritually connected" during a session, to be in constant dialogue with the Divine, both praying for the client and listening for guidance at all times. Here is where Brother Lawrence's discipline of practicing the presence of God is particularly useful. Tending to this level of intimacy outside of one's sessions will help one to maintain close contact with the Divine while one is in them. And vice versa—becoming adept at the push-and-pull of speaking and listening to the Divine during a session, when the pressure is really on, can help one maintain such conscious contact when the pressure is off, as well. In fact, any degree of expertise in one's prayer life is going to help one be a better spiritual guide since good communication skills are an asset regardless of where one is or what one is doing.

Giving alms. The third pillar of Islam is almsgiving, the setting aside of a percentage of a person's income to be spent on the poor, widows, orphans, or other charitable needs. It was very important to Muhammad to avoid the disparity between the rich and the poor he had seen in Mecca, and thus he made it incumbent upon every Muslim to give generously to those in greater need. This is an important discipline in that it encourages responsible distribution of resources, is a constant prod toward compassion, and reminds those of means that their wealth is a gift to them that can be withdrawn at any time.

Islam has a complicated system to determine how much should be given. One is expected to give one-fortieth of one's monetary gain, but 10 percent of one's actual agricultural produce. And when it comes to livestock, forget it—it's way too involved to relate, here. There are also two different ways one should give: there is both a tax for the poor that is regulated, and voluntary giving (which, though no less compulsory, is done on a sort of honor system).

Other religious traditions also emphasize charitable giving. The ancient Israelites were commanded to set aside a tenth part of all their income for the support of the priestly tribe, who tended to the spiritual health of the Jewish people. Christians continued this tradition, encouraging believers to give 10 percent of their income to the church to support its ministry, which usually includes some form of support for the poor. Many Christians are less strict about the percentage, although some, such as the Mormons, demand 10 percent of one's gross income (and require a copy of one's tax forms to prove the amount!). Much more lenient is the Community of Christ (formerly known as the Reorganized Church of Jesus Christ of Latter Day Saints—those that did not immigrate to Utah after the death of Joseph Smith, Jr.), for whom a proper tithe is 10 percent of all that is *left over* after one's basic financial commitments have been met. Some Episcopal churches today suggest a "modern tithe" of 5 percent of one's take-home pay. In the end, everyone must decide for him- or herself what feels like a proper amount.

American politics has, of late, been talking about "faith-based" programs, encouraging basic welfare needs to be met at the local, voluntary level instead of being mandated and controlled by the state. If everyone kept a strict discipline of almsgiving, such rhetoric would be quite correct, and the needs of all could be met by the freely given donations of money and time. As stated before, however, spiritual disciplines are of limited value when coerced (it may help the person in need, but does little for the arm-twisted giver), and the amount that is freely given is woefully inadequate to meet the need.

Though the person given to no doubt benefits, it is the benefit to the giver—the one practicing this particular spiritual discipline—that we are primarily concerned with here. Giving remains an important discipline for the soul. To give a portion of my income reminds me that I am not working for my own selfish gain, but that I have a responsibility toward the community of which I am a part. My wealth (such as it is) does not benefit me alone, but should benefit, in some way, however small, everyone around me as well. It reminds me that my life may be required of me tonight, and all my accumulated goods will not benefit me in the grave. It also keeps before me the reality of those for whom compassion is required; I am not an island, but the poor and dispossessed are also a part of me.

Toward this end, we do well to recommend this discipline to our clients. There are many ways to give alms, and all of them are useful. The most prevalent is the giving of a portion of one's income to a place of worship. Not only does this support the ministry of the church, synagogue, temple, or mosque to those in the neighborhood, but most places also sponsor some sort of direct outreach to the poor, whether through on-site programs (such as soup kitchens or food distribution) or through cooperative giving efforts (where many houses of worship pool their resources to have a greater impact upon a specific population).

Other nonprofits, though, should not be overlooked. Any group that works to make the world a better, more just place is worthy of support. Whether it is an organization that buys up land to keep it free of development, one that tapes volunteers reading books for the blind, or one that rescues unwanted companion animals; giving to such groups should not be neglected.

It should be noted here that not everyone has money to spare, regardless of how compassionate he or she might be. But money is not the only way to give; volunteering one's time is another way of giving alms that is, in many ways, even more personally rewarding. There is a Japanese school of psychotherapy holding as its basic tenet that people who are suffering from severe neuroses suffer less when they are volunteering their time to assist those less fortunate than they. Seeing the suffering of others puts their own pain in perspective, and they become less self-absorbed and focused on their own problems. And very often, the hands-on experience of helping others gives their lives meaning that was lacking before, bringing with it a sense of being needed, an increased self-esteem, and a greater sense of general well-being.

I believe there is something to this method of therapy—giving of one's time and energy in the service of others is healing to the soul. I have even suggested it to clients, especially those who were suffering psychologically. Unfortunately, most of them have been too depressed and self-absorbed to venture out to even find a venue for such service. This is indeed a difficult hurdle to overcome for such people, but as anyone who has ever volunteered time in this way can attest, the rewards are substantial.

Fasting. Abstaining from food as a way to intensify prayer and to purify oneself, or as an ascetic discipline, has a long history in religious observance. In Islam, believers fast for the entire month of Ramadan to celebrate Allah's giving of the Qur'an to humankind. This fast is not terribly rigorous, and is observed only during daylight hours. That means that a person can have a hefty breakfast before daybreak, and dinner at sundown, so long as nothing is eaten during the day. Harder, however, is fasting from all liquids during the day. Sexual intercourse, too, is banned during daylight hours.

To what end do Muslims eschew food, drink, and the occasional "afternoon delight"? Traditional sources believe that it disciplines both body and soul, serves to remind those who have plenty of food what it feels like to have none, and encourages solidarity among all those who profess the Muslim faith.

Hindu ascetics have likewise lauded the usefulness of fasting. For them it is part of a constellation of ascetic practices that emphasizes the ephemerality (and illusory nature) of the body, and helps to focus the mind in meditation toward the final goal of liberation. The Buddha eschewed the practice as harmful to the body, but not all fasting is as rigorous or dangerous as that which the Buddha encountered.

In the Christian tradition, there are two main seasons of fasting, Advent (where one awaits the coming of Christ) and Lent (a period of purification prior to Easter). Lenten fasting is the more rigorous, but even then one does not abstain from all food, but only from certain foods, usually delicacies or foods (or drinks) that are pleasurable but unnecessary (such as chocolate or cognac).

Other traditions also have traditions of fasting, and each of them has found ways to temper the practice so that it provides the most spiritual benefit with the least amount of physical harm (though each tradition also boasts its extremists).

Fasting may seem to most folks today to be an antiquated, even quaint, practice, with little practical application. Yet this is a form of cultural snobbery of which we should be careful. Fasting continues to be a useful tool for spiritual guidance, even if not always wrapped in its traditional guise.

When Sally came to her spiritual director, Margaret, she presented her primary difficulty as her lack of a husband. Margaret, who had been widowed fifteen years ago, and had remained unmarried since, was personally skeptical as to whether Sally's spiritual conflicts were related to her unwilling solitude. Sally dated frequently, and a sadness came over her whenever she spoke about it. Finally, Margaret presented her with a challenge.

"I'd like to suggest a spiritual discipline for you that is going to seem very hard. But if you can do it, I think it might give you some insight into the problems you are having."

"I'll try anything," Sally promised.

"I'd like to suggest that you fast."

"From food?"

"From dating."

Sally looked at her as if she had just sprouted a second head. "What, are you kidding me?"

"No, far from it. I'd like you to go home and pray about it. If you get the feeling that God is in this—then do it."

"What, forever?" Sally was still incredulous.

"No, of course not. But, for six months, say. What do you think?"

"I think I'll think about it," Sally said curtly.

"But will you pray about it?" Margaret asked.

"Okay, I'll pray about it."

Sally did pray about it, and with a heaviness that Margaret had not seen before, she agreed to the fast. It was torture at first, as Sally didn't know who she was when not in relationship with a man. She had to face herself truly alone, and to discover who she was as an individual.

A formidable depression ensued, which worried Margaret, who began to wonder if she had done the right thing. Margaret felt strangely comforted when praying for Sally, however, and she somehow trusted that the Divine was doing its work.

About two months into the fast, a shift occurred in Sally. She became more sober, grounded, and intentional about her spiritual life than Margaret had ever seen. The sessions were no longer pervaded by sadness, but had turned into poignant and holy meditations on mortality and identity as Sally confronted deep issues that she had for years avoided.

After the six months were up, Sally did go back to dating, but she did it as a different person. She dated fewer men, less often, and often went for months between beaus. Her dating rarely came up in session after that, except for incidents that had direct bearing upon her spiritual wrestlings.

Fasting can be a powerful tool for spiritual guidance, especially when clients agree to fast from something with which they have an obsessive relationship. Too often these things can serve to mask other issues and can obfuscate our intimacy with the Divine. Fasting can help us clear away the cobwebs, see our relationships to people, situations, food, and other substances with greater clarity. Far from an antiquated practice, in an age of mindless consumption, mindful abstinence can be a blessed source of wisdom.

Pilgrimage. Every Muslim is encouraged to visit Mecca at least once in his or her life. Called the *hajj*, this pilgrimage must be performed in the twelfth month of the year, and be accompanied by various rituals in order to "count" as far as satisfying one's obligation. Various sites between Medina and Mecca are visited, but the highlight of the journey is prayer around the Kaaba, a large, black, boxlike structure housing an enormous black rock, which tradition says was a gift from the angel Gabriel to Abraham (or *Ibrahim*, in Arabic).

Pilgrims go through a purification process to prepare themselves for the journey. Men shave their heads and everyone dons white robes, which serve to remind them that all are equal in the sight of Allah. No jewelry, perfume, or other trappings of wealth or social standing are permitted.

While pilgrimage is incumbent upon all Muslims, the practice has lost currency in Christianity. Pilgrimages to holy sites used to be very common for Christians, but fewer and fewer people are doing them as conscious spiritual practices these days. Many Christians still visit Israel to see "where Jesus walked," or Rome, hoping to catch a glimpse of the pope, but such journeys are often mixtures of tourism and devotion. Few see the journey itself as a catalyst for spiritual transformation, but this is exactly what it is meant to be.

The pilgrimage is a metaphor for the winding journey of one's life. Many people of faith see their lives as having a spiritual center, a transcendent end point, which the pilgrim's destination represents. The journey toward the holy site is the journey toward Divinity, the time spent there is time resting in the bosom of the Holy, and the journey home again carries the wisdom one has found back to inform and transform the rest of life. Pilgrimage reminds us that life goes on outside our circle of familiarity, liberates us from the petty concerns of daily living, and reorients our lives toward the Divine.

Labyrinth walks are tiny pilgrimages, and can serve the same purpose in miniature. They can serve as preparation for the pilgrim, and can help bring to memory the graces of the journey once one has returned home, as well.

In the less-affluent East, pilgrimages are still quite popular and have lost little of their spiritual impact. Hindus still flock to the holy city of Benares to bathe in the holy Ganges river, and Buddhists continue to make their way to Bodhgaya to sit near the Bodhi Tree, where the Buddha first achieved enlightenment.

After spending twelve years as an Old Catholic priest, I felt moved to make a pilgrimage to Utrecht, Holland, the archiepiscopal see of the Old Catholic Communion. I spent a sleepless night before visiting this ancient city, and my heart pounded as I boarded the train. Soon, however, my companions and I found ourselves standing outside St. Gertrude's Cathedral, the Old Catholic equivalent of Canterbury or Vatican City.

As I wandered the aisles of the cathedral, I was overwhelmed with emotion. It was a stunningly beautiful building, where, I knew, the archbishop of Utrecht presides regularly over the Divine Liturgy, and by extension, all we who are of this peculiar ecclesial lineage.

Visiting the many museums and "hidden churches" that bear witness to Holland's catholic history, I felt a connection to history and a continuity of ministry I had not experienced before. I brought a little bit of Utrecht back to Berkeley in my heart, and when I stand to say Mass week after week, I do it not as an isolated priest, but as part of a great stream of witnesses whose testimony and wisdom continue to have bearing in my words and actions. In this way my pilgrimage was transformative not only for me personally, but for my ministry to the many people I touch here in Berkeley as well.

Pilgrimages can be just as life-changing for our clients. Like any spiritual practice, a pilgrimage, when made with prayerful intention, can reorient our life, expose myths about our own identities, and connect us powerfully with the great stream of history. "Religion" literally means to "reconnect," and a pilgrimage can facilitate a person's reconnection with the Divine, with tradition, and with his or her own soul like few other disciplines.

My friend Daniel and his wife Elizabeth participated in a most unusual pilgrimage a few years ago. Together with the Buddhist Peace Fellowship, they walked from Auschwitz to Hiroshima, chanting for peace the entire way. None who walked with them returned unchanged, and few who encountered them on their journey, or who heard their story afterward, were unmoved by it. In their case, pilgrimage served not only as a personal spiritual discipline, but in fact was itself an act of prayerful protest that changed not only *their* world, but *the* world.

Even short pilgrimages to places that have personal resonance can be helpful, and the destinations do not always have to be specifically religious.

Who am I to say that my mother's journey to visit Elvis's grave at Graceland was not a spiritually significant event for her, or that someone struggling to affirm the holiness of his queer identity would not benefit from visiting the site of the Stonewall riots? Certainly Selma has gained the status of a holy site for those commemorating the civil rights movement in the United States, and pilgrimages to such sites are not uncommon. Nor are they unimportant. Just as each of us has his or her own journey, and each of them is sacred, each of us has pilgrimage sites holy only to us, the journeys to which we ignore at our own peril.

Other Practices

Rule of Life. Soon after Christian monks and nuns began living in community together, the need for some document which spelled out what was expected of them in terms of both behavior and spiritual practice became obvious. Every order compiled a "rule," outlining boundaries and responsibilities incumbent upon each of its members. A rule can prescribe everything from how and when the community prays, to how guests are to be received, to what time everyone goes to bed.

Rules are not just helpful for monks and nuns, however. Many people who want to be intentional about their spiritual lives will create a rule for themselves. Such rules are not a prohibitive list of "don'ts" but usually a list of "do's," outlining those practices a person wishes to commit to on a daily basis. Creating a rule can help a client be clear about exactly the kind of practice he or she wants to do, when and how often it will be performed, and how it fits in with the rest of his or her life.

Sandra was just getting ready to go on retreat, and had made a last-minute appointment with me before she went. She was headed out to a nearby monastery for a week of rest and prayer. "I wanted to talk to you before I go," she said, breathlessly, dropping into a chair. "I will only have a few days and I don't want to waste them. What should I do when I get there?"

I asked her what she wanted to get out of the retreat. "Well, I want to rest, that's for sure. And I want to meditate every day, and I want to read that Thich Nhat Hahn book I've been carrying around with me for a month."

"Okay," I said, "Let's outline your day from the time you get up. What time is breakfast at the monastery?"

Sandra was an early riser, so as we talked through her day, the following rule took shape:

6:00 A.M.	Wake up, shower
6:30 A.M.	Walk the labyrinth
7:00 A.M.	Mass
8:00 A.M.	Breakfast
9:00 A.M.	Writing
11:00 A.M.	Free time
12:00 P.M.	Lunch
1:00 P.M.	Nap
3:00 P.M.	Reading
5:00 P.M.	Meditation
6:00 P.M.	Supper
7:00 P.M.	Leisure time

When she returned, I asked her how the rule had worked out. "Great, more or less." She smiled. "I followed it every day, but every day I made little changes. I'm just not good at following rules." Then she laughed.

I laughed with her. "Well, nobody is holding your feet to the fire, and no one is concerned about whether you do it perfectly or not. Was it helpful as a guide?"

"Oh, yeah!" she said. "It really helped me focus. I never woke up with that feeling of vertigo, you know, that 'what the hell do I do now?' feeling. I always knew what I was going to do next, even if I chose in the moment not to do it. It . . . held me."

A rule of life can be simple or complex. If the idea is new to you, or to a client, it is best to keep it simple. The last thing you want to do is to construct a rule so rigorous that you can't possibly meet its demands, because then you will end up feeling like a failure. It's best to plan for success, keeping the rule to the bare minimum of what is both necessary and desirable for you. You want it to provide structure, not strictures. Just like a visit to the salad bar at Sizzler, our spiritual eyes may be bigger than our stomachs, and it is easier to load up on more than we can handle. But if we keep the commitments simple and reasonable, it can be a great aid to our practice.

The rule can also change as you or your client grows and changes.

A rule may need to be revised every couple of months or so, perhaps even weekly, as you or your client feel your way into it. Eventually you will discover the "sweet spot": just enough structure to help you do what you want to do, not so much that it becomes a burden. As a spiritual guide, you can help your client by checking in with her or him about how things are going with her or his rule. Some people like to be held accountable, others would rather not be reminded, especially if they are not sticking with it. You'll know pretty quickly which sort your clients are. And if the rule isn't working for them, and they don't feel like revising it, just drop it. Structure is simply not everybody's thing.

Holy Reading. For some of us, this discipline is the easiest—and for some, the hardest. Those of us of a literary bent will probably feel like this discipline is cheating—it doesn't feel like a discipline at all. We would read no matter what, and since many of us are fascinated by all things spiritual and religious, much of what we read falls into this category anyway.

Every faith has a tradition of holy reading. In Islam, believers are expected to read the Qur'an and its many commentaries written over the centuries. Buddhists read the sutras and their commentaries. The Hindus have more scriptures than any one person could ever possibly read in one lifetime, not to mention all the commentaries on them. Jews read the Torah, and compare it with the arguments in the Talmud. Christians read the Bible, the church fathers, and the writings of the saints and mystics. Each tradition has books that fall within an accepted canon of scripture, and many more books that are not considered scripture, but are nevertheless counted as valuable reading.

All of these are good choices for holy reading. In addition, each tradition will have contemporary authors writing books that popularize their traditions and make them accessible and relevant to daily living. Authors such as Pema Chodron, Ken Wilber, Jack Kornfield, David Cooper, Matthew Fox, and many others write books for today's seekers, and provide helpful introductions to the wisdom of their respective traditions.

Reading theology is a spiritual path all its own, and is instrumental to *jnana yoga*, or the path of knowledge. Even if one's favorite reading tends more toward mysteries or science fiction novels, having at least one spirituality book going, which one dips into at least once per day, is a good discipline to keep. For some of us, this is no problem—the problem is often limiting the number of books in our "active" pile to a number we can actually read. Again, sometimes our spiritual appetites are often bigger than our actual capacities for consumption.

For some people, those with dyslexia or learning disorders, holy reading can indeed seem like a burden. It can still be a valuable discipline for such folks, but the selection of material will be of primary importance. The point is not to force people to read, but to provide meat for the soul. Many publishing companies have issued daily devotionals, little paperbacks of exactly 365 pages, one for each day of the year. Each page contains a quotation from the scriptures of one or many traditions, followed by a brief meditation explicating the text, and concluding with a prayer or affirmation to help the reader integrate the day's wisdom.

Other books, such as Bear & Company's *Meditations With . . .* series are also perfect for people who struggle with reading. These books present a single pithy quotation per page culled from the writings of a world mystic, rendered in modern English. Each page takes only a short time to read, even for those who do not read fast, but each quote is carefully selected to pack a real punch. One quote is worthy of a full day's meditation.

The Hard Work of Submission

Part of Muhammad's genius was his insight into the human condition—the absolute tyranny of the ego, and the need to liberate one's self from its control through submission to the divine will. This is indeed as hard as it sounds, and the many disciplines prescribed by Islam and other traditions are not shortcuts, but ready tools at hand for those prepared to do the hard work of spiritual transformation.

There is no lazy person's path to enlightenment, and anyone professing to have one is simply not to be trusted. Just as there is no free lunch, there is also no free liberation. No one can force someone to do the work, but sooner or later, whether in this life or another, most of us will roll up our sleeves and get down to business. Standing up for our beliefs, prayer and meditation, giving to the poor, abstaining from food and favorite pleasures, going on pilgrimage, creating a rule of life, and doing holy reading can, when used with moderation and responsibility, assist one on the path to spiritual maturity. Of course, this is not an exhaustive list. Every tradition honors some form of each of the categories we have discussed, plus others unique to it.

As spiritual guides it is important for us to have firsthand knowledge of many such disciplines, so that we can recognize when one or the other might be helpful for our clients. The greater *jihad*, the battle that takes place within each of us, is more important than any exterior conflict, because it is within the human soul that the salvation of the world resides, not in weapons and armor, but in the ability to say, "not my will, but thine."

9

Sikhism and the Interfaith Path

M any of us who practice spiritual guidance from an interfaith perspective were moved to do so because of our experiences, both positive and negative, of many traditions. We see that there is much of value in every tradition we study, but we also see that the exclusive claims of religions in their traditional form have been the cause of much suffering, cruelty, and even bloodshed in the world, all in the name of the gods.

This has caused some of us to open ourselves to the truths beyond the tradition that we personally practice, and for others it has inspired an eclectic approach to spirituality that draws primarily not from one tradition, but from many. While traditionalists of most religions are extremely uncomfortable with such an orientation (just try explaining the idea of "interfaith ministry" to a Fundamentalist of any religion, and watch the fireworks that ensue!), such openness and eclecticism seem to be moving increasingly into the mainstream.

It just seems common sense that the Divine would not abandon any peoples, and would speak to them throughout the ages, utilizing whatever images, metaphors, and stories are familiar and efficacious in their cultures. As interfaith spiritual guides, we assume the Divine continues to work in just this way—meeting people wherever they are, using the experiences, stories, and cultures familiar to them to nudge them toward wholeness and community. If you are reading this book, you are probably sympathetic to this perspective, but you may be surprised to know that it is not a modern phenomenon. The roots of a truly interfaith approach to spirituality go all the way back to the fifteenth century, to the story of a cattle driver named Nanak.

Nanak was born in Talwandi, a tiny village in what is now Pakistan. His father was an accountant for their Muslim landlord, and his mother was a pious Hindu woman. A headstrong boy who always followed his own drummer, Nanak was impatient with religious rituals, and despised the Hindu caste system that ordered society. He also hated going to school, and preferred to lose himself in contemplation. His father, tired of trying to coerce his education, finally sent him off to watch the herds where he could lose himself in contemplation and still be of some use to the family.

Nanak really tried to be a proper Hindu, but so much of the tradition was repellent to him that he eventually abandoned it. Then he tried Islam on for size, but finally decided that it did not quite fit him, either. Each had so many rules, so many barriers that separated people from one another. If God was One, how could there be so many different religions, so many different castes—how could there be acceptable people and not-acceptable people? Nanak wandered after the herds and pondered these things.

Then, when he was twenty-eight years old, an amazing thing happened. Leaving the herd and his fellow herdsmen to take a bath in a nearby stream, Nanak was gone a long time. This was not unusual, and his workmates assumed he was simply lost in one of his reveries. But by nightfall he still had not returned. They went out searching for him, to no avail. Finally, they decided he must have drowned, and gave him up for dead.

Just then, after three days absence, Nanak emerged from the wild—but he was not the same young man who had gone off to bathe. The story he told his relieved friends and family was incredible. He told them that while he was standing in the river, he was overwhelmed by the presence of the Divine. A cup filled with sacred nectar was offered to him, and a voice commanded him, "This cup, Nanak, is the adoration of my Name. Drink it, for I am with you and bless you. I will smile with favor upon anyone who remembers you. So go, rejoice in my Name, and teach others to do so as well. This is your calling."[25]

As the vision passed, Nanak came up out of the water and spoke the immortal words: "There is no Hindu. There is no Muslim." When he related the story to his friends, he explained, "God is neither Hindu nor Muslim, and the path I follow is God's."[26] Nanak was not denying the truth of these religions, only the exclusiveness with which many of their devotees held them. God could be found in Islam and Hinduism, but the Divine was limited to neither of them. Divinity transcended every tradition, and every tradition revealed a way of being faithful and of reaching spiritual fulfillment.

True to his calling, Nanak took his message to the streets. He dressed in a mishmash of styles drawn from the traditional wardrobes of both Hindus and Muslims. Instead of writing laws and doctrines, Nanak wrote love songs to the Divine, and traveled far and wide with his Muslim friend Mardana, who played the rebec while Nanak sang. He sang to peoples of every tribe, every caste, every faith, making no distinctions between them, but offering to all his songs of love for the Divine. He played at mosques and temples; for Buddhist sanghas and Sufi schools; at festivals and in the marketplaces.

He told Muslims to be faithful to the Qur'an, and charged Hindus to be true to their traditions, but also preached that the truth of the Divine transcended every system of belief. He preached an egalitarianism that was threatening to some, for he was fiercely critical of the caste system, and insisted that men and women were equals in the sight of the Divine, and ought to be in the eyes of the law. Although he met with some resistance, overwhelmingly Nanak succeeded in bringing people together wherever he went. Hindus, Muslims, Christians, and Buddhists alike crowded around to hear him sing, forgetting for a while their differences, and finding themselves inspired by his vision of their common humanity and their equal standing before Divinity.

Soon, people began to follow after him. They adopted his teaching, and began to proclaim his interfaith message themselves. They called themselves "Sikhs," which means, "disciples."

Sikhism after Nanak

Just before he died, Nanak appointed one of his disciples, named Lahina, to succeed him as guru and leader of the fledgling Sikh community. He renamed him "Angad," which means "part of my own body." Like Nanak, Angad also wrote songs and poems, but he wrote them in Nanak's name. As a later guru would write, "And now the writ of Angad ran instead of Nanak's; for the Light was the same, the Way the same, only the body had changed." Most of the gurus in succession continued to write poetry.

The fifth guru, Arjan, set about the task of compiling a collection of these songs, to preserve them for the community, and to weed out the authentic poems from the pseudepigraphal. Since all the poems were meant to be sung, he arranged them musically into thirty-two sections. Within each section, poems were listed in the order of the guru who composed them. But songs by the Sikh gurus were not the only ones selected for inclusion. The sacred text also included works by Hindu and Muslim mystics—Kabir has 292 songs included. The collection was called the Granth (Book). He also had a beautiful temple erected to house the book when the collection was complete.

Around the turn of the eighteenth century, the tenth guru, Gobind, announced that there would be no more human gurus after his death—instead, the Granth itself would become the guru. So modest was Guru Gobind that he did not even allow his own poetry, which is just as lovely as many of the selections in the Granth, to be included. The Dasam Granth collects his works, and it is highly esteemed, even if it is not regarded as "the guru."

For the first century or so after Guru Nanak, the Sikhs continued his ministry of inspiring people of different faiths to see their similarities rather than their differences. The songs of Nanak and his successors continued to move people of various traditions, and the Sikhs stood as a witness to the common Spirit at the heart of all things.

But as the Sikhs grew in number and began to develop their own traditions, they came to be seen not as an interfaith movement, but as a religion unto themselves. The Muslim government that ruled India at that time saw them as a threat, and they imprisoned and killed the fifth guru, Arjan. The oppression became so intense that the sixth guru, Hargobind, eschewed the traditional dress at his consecration, and instead came to the event dressed as a warrior. He bade the Sikhs abandon their vegetarianism and develop strong bodies that would be formidable in battle.

The ninth guru, Tegh Bahadur, challenged the Muslims' practice of forcing Hindus to convert by the sword, and was himself executed in 1675. His son was Guru Gobind, the last of the gurus, who instituted the Khalsa, the Order of the Pure. Those inducted took the surname "Singh," which means "lion," and wore five emblems of their order: uncut hair, a comb to keep it neat, a bracelet of steel, a variety of trousers worn by soldiers at the time, and a sword. They also swore to defend the helpless and fight oppression.

This militant tradition continued to be strong in Sikhism, and during the English occupation of India, the Sikh regiments were highly esteemed by the British. To this day, most Sikhs retain the emblems of the Kalsa, and usually wear a turban to manage their long hair.

An Interfaith Vision

Though circumstances forced the Sikh community to consolidate and to some degree insulate themselves from the cultures that oppressed and threatened them, the interfaith vision of Guru Nanak continues to inspire Sikhs and non-Sikhs alike. It is a tragic irony that a message intended to unite all faiths in their common humanity and openness to the Divine was forced to become just another religion competing for converts. Though it was probably unavoidable; in becoming just another faith among many, Sikhism lost its prophetic edge, and with it, some of its ability to inspire people of all faiths.

This is a strong caution to those of us who do interfaith work today not to try to codify just what is or is not "interfaith." Once one begins to articulate an "interfaith theology," one is essentially setting up a new dogma and robbing interfaith work of its power to reach across traditions, to unite people, and to speak prophetically to both sacred and secular authority.

Yet the subsequent history of the Sikhs as a separate religion does not invalidate the mystical, unitive vision of Nanak and the other early Sikh mystics. With them, we who do interfaith ministry can affirm the words of the Granth:

> Countless are the ways of meditation,
> and countless the avenue to love,
> Countless the ways of worship,
> and countless the paths of austerity and sacrifice.
> Countless the texts, and countless the Vedic reciters,
> Countless the yogis turning away from the world,
> Countless the devout reflecting on virtue and knowledge,
> Countless the pious, and countless the patrons,

Countless the warriors, faces scarred by iron
Countless the sages sunk in silent trance.
How can I express the Primal Power?
I cannot offer myself to you even once.
. . . Countless are Your names and countless Your places,
Unreachable and unfathomable are Your countless spheres.
. . . Only that which pleases You is good.
You are forever constant, Formless One.[27]

Those of us who feel called to interfaith spiritual guidance know in our souls that there is no one religious tradition that has a monopoly on truth. We see the smile of the Divine in the ecstatic dance of Shiva, in the quiet ebb and flow of the Tao, in the serene posture of the Buddha, in the healing touch of the Christ. We hear eternal wisdom in the commandments of Moses, in the call to prayer of the muezzin, in the mystical poetry of the Granth. We seek to honor this truth wherever it may be found, and to help our clients live in conscious relationship with divinity, in whatever form they recognize it.

The idea of spiritually companioning someone of another faith is a relatively new idea. As a modern movement in the spiritual direction community, we see its beginnings in the mid-1970s, when Protestant Christians began coming to Catholics for spiritual direction. Then, to everyone's surprise, those same Protestants began signing up for training at Catholic institutions. Soon, Catholics began receiving direction from Protestants. This was about all the innovation people could handle right away, and many people were uncomfortable with such "interfaith" work. But just as people were adjusting to this ecumenical turn, Jewish people began to take an interest in the ministry. Then the odd Buddhist started showing up. While some continued to protest, the dam had broken—the ministry of formal, professional spiritual guidance was not just for Christians anymore. Jews began companioning Christians, Unitarians companioned Buddhists, and Sufis started to companion Wiccans. And all of them started coming to be trained. This book is the result of precisely this explosion of the professional ministry of spiritual guidance out of the Christian tradition and into the spiritual practices of peoples of all faiths.

While this is a grand and marvelous shift, interfaith spiritual guidance is not always as easy as it sounds. Many of us come from traditions that are exclusive by nature ("our way is the only way"), and even though we have consciously rejected such spiritual imperialism, many unconscious assumptions and prejudices about other faiths continue to have an impact on us.

How can we do spiritual guidance in a truly interfaith way, honoring our own understanding and at the same time validating the experiences and beliefs of our clients, which may, in fact, be very different from our own? How do we walk the same tightrope that Nanak did, affirming in one breath the value and validity of diverse traditions, while in the next proclaiming, "there is no Hindu, no Muslim," no Christian, no Jew, no Wiccan, no Buddhist? Interfaith ministry celebrates a unity in diversity that affirms the access of every people to the Divine, through whatever images, stories, and ideas are meaningful for them. But how do we do this work faithfully, without letting our own traditions, our own faith stories, and our own internal paradigms get in the way?

In some ways it is not that different from spiritual guidance within the same faith tradition—for we all have differing experiences, different journeys, different ways of understanding our faiths. But because of the incredible volume of information needed to grasp the religions of the world—the sheer kaleidoscope of images, myths, beliefs, and assumptions—interfaith spiritual guidance comes with its own set of challenges.

I have discerned three methods—three modes—for doing interfaith spiritual guidance. By selecting the appropriate mode, this system allows someone with limited experience with other faiths a way to successfully companion those of other faith traditions, while also providing models for those with a more advanced understanding.

Mode I: Sharing Wisdom

When Kay approached Donna for spiritual direction several years ago, she did not know very much about her. Kay was a Jewish woman who attended a Conservative synagogue. Aware that Donna was a Roman Catholic, Kay was open to the possibility that Donna might have a valid spiritual journey as well, and, to a limited extent, was open to the insights of Catholic spirituality. They agreed that they would not try to convert one another, and when they sat together, they did so as Jew and Catholic, respectively. Kay was fearful at first, when Donna suggested reading one of the medieval mystics ("It's all so Catholic!" she complained after her first foray), but she soon warmed to them and acknowledged that they did indeed have something to teach her about the spiritual journey. Donna encouraged her to maintain a devotional practice congruent with her tradition, and to increase her involvement in her local synagogue.

This is the most popular mode of interfaith spiritual guidance. In this mode, spiritual guide and client each sit securely in their respective faith traditions, utilizing wisdom from each freely—not trying to convert, but respecting each person's path as distinctly his or hers. For this reason, each party should agree that valid spiritual paths exist outside his or her own. Like Guru Nanak and his Muslim rebec player, Mardana, who traveled the length and breadth of India together singing songs of divine love, spiritual guides in this mode encourage their clients in their home traditions, and likewise proudly embrace their own, even while embarking on a common journey of spiritual discovery.

Although it is possible to accompany someone of another tradition having no knowledge of the client's native faith, it is far better to have an understanding of the major principles of that faith tradition. Misunderstandings about religion are legion; misconceptions abound and can have disastrous results in direction. For instance, a Baptist spiritual guide should not assume his Catholic client believes he has to work his way into heaven, a common notion in Baptist circles. The director has some responsibility to do basic research on a client's spiritual tradition, as well as to be teachable during sessions.

In this mode, the guide should listen closely for elements in the client's faith tradition that have charged significance that the guide might be missing due to his or her unfamiliarity with the tradition. The guide should be liberal with questions about unknowns in a client's tradition.

Spiritual guides should also feel free to offer analogies and anecdotes from their own faith tradition. Since religious feeling is fairly consistent throughout humankind, such analogical experimentation can help a guide understand and empathize with a client's religious experience, and the director should not hesitate to employ it.

A particular pitfall to this approach is the (often unconscious) assumption of the superiority of one's own tradition, which can afflict any spiritual guide. Most will deny this cognitively, but it is the dearness of the familiar that can—and most often does—betray us.

Mode II: Paradigm Shifting

When Mary first wrote to Chris requesting e-mail spiritual direction, he was delighted. She presented herself as a "liberal Zen Buddhist," and had gleaned from the writings on his website that he might be a suitable spiritual guide for her. Chris was a Unitarian Universalist humanist, but had been sitting za-zen for years, and in fact, had spent several months in a Buddhist monastic community. He felt he knew the "lay of the land" for Buddhists pretty well, and was well-read in the tradition. Whenever he came to the keyboard to companion Mary, he consciously left his own universe behind and entered the Zen Buddhist world completely. It was tempting to bring a "picnic basket" of wisdom from other traditions with him (and he did, in fact, sneak in an item or two now and then), but he was largely successful at checking his own paradigm at the door and entering fully into hers.

In this mode, Mode II, the spiritual guide "surfs" from one paradigm to another, entering completely into the worldview of the client. The guide, essentially, "puts on" the religious universe of the client the way Mr. Rogers puts on his sweater, leaving his or her own religious tradition on a peg in the hall.

Mode II is much more demanding on the spiritual guide than the first mode. To do this effectively, the guide needs to have a nearly encyclopedic knowledge of the client's faith tradition, and at least some firsthand knowl-edge as well. Because of this, a spiritual guide is going to be limited in those he or she can direct in this mode. But if one is a convert from one tradition to another (and assuming one is on good terms with one's faith of origin), or has over time studied many religions, this can be a very effective mode indeed.

The assumptions of this mode are that while religious experience is common to all peoples, the cultural clothes in which that experience finds expression (the religious tradition) are to some extent arbitrary. A spiritual guide conversant in many traditions—and comfortable with them—can enter a string of conflicting universes with minimal vertigo.

Trouble spots to look for in this mode include assuming more knowl-edge about a tradition than one actually has, and the possibly false assump-tion that one can adequately empathize with religious experiences in garb with which we are not adequately familiar or comfortable. Another dan-ger is forgetting which room of the cosmological house one is in and "slipping back" into another paradigm, especially one's preferred paradigm. This mode demands that we remain with our clients in their own spiritual universes, speaking to them in their native religious languages, and illustrating our points with stories and examples largely from their own traditions.

Another pitfall is a guide's possible neglect of the spiritual disciplines of his or her own tradition once he or she has achieved such an inner sense of religious relativity. Professional responsibility demands that we give plenty of attention to our own spiritual disciplines and commitment to our spiritual communities, even if these are acquired in a variety of settings.

Mode III: Beyond Traditions

Gary had walked the mystic's path for some time, going from Roman Catholic practice to Episcopalian to Baptist and back to the Anglicans in his spiritual journey. He read widely in the world's religions, and had come to regard many faiths to be valid paths to liberation. He struggled with which tradition to participate in, when something strange and mysterious happened. The Goddess came to him in a dream and claimed him for her own. Discerning that this was a true sign, Gary devoted himself to the study of Wicca, the old way of the Goddess.

Gary felt he had come home, and his spiritual journey kicked into high gear when he began to work toward his initiations. He is now a Wiccan priest, and the first Wiccan hospital chaplain in his area.

Since Rebecca had studied Wicca formally, she might have chosen to journey with Gary from one paradigm to another, as in Mode II. But instead, though Gary's religious practice changed dramatically, he still viewed the world from an essentially interfaith perspective, acknowledging many valid spiritual paths. Consequently, their conversations drew from Taoist, Christian, Buddhist, and many other spiritual traditions, in addition to Wicca. They met at that place where there is no name, but every name, no way but every way, no distinction yet myriad expressions. They met in a place outside of any one tradition, but informed by many. This is the perspective of Nanak's original vision, which moved him to declare, "There is no Hindu, there is no Muslim," yet inspired him to embrace the wisdom of both of these—and other—traditions.

This path is the rarest of the modes, as it requires both the spiritual guide and the client to be knowledgeable of many spiritual traditions, or at least eager to explore them. It assumes that both guide and client have renounced any of the exclusive claims of their chosen traditions, and that both can come from an interfaith orientation. This mode is for unabashed mystics, who can affirm and embrace the Divine in whatever cultural or religious guise they may encounter. In this mode, all religious traditions are honored, but none are revered uncritically. All of them are plumbed for wisdom, but none are taken literally. Like Nanak, spiritual guides and clients operating from such a place of mystical unity can affirm,

> Worlds below worlds, worlds above worlds,
> Tired of seeking their limits, the Vedas say one thing
> Arabic scriptures speak of eighteen thousand worlds
>   traced to one source.
> If It could be written, It would be written,
>   but all writing passes away.
> Nanak says, praise the Great who alone knows Itself. (*Beloved*, 55)

A danger of this Mode is its headiness. Mystics can get lost in the One and lose interest in other aspects of their lives. Spiritual guides can help such mystics remember that the One includes their mundane lives as well. Disconnected from a tradition, people with an eclectic, interfaith perspective can languish with no spiritual discipline, rule of life, or community. The Benedictine monastic tradition lends insight to the need to balance contemplation with hard work and close community, and Buddhist mindfulness practice encourages seekers to ground themselves in a *sangha* (spiritual community), where needs for fellowship, accountability, and service can be met.

A potential danger is the spiritual guide's own level of comfort with religious elements that such an eclectic client might bring to a session. If a client senses that a spiritual guide has a prejudice against, say, Hinduism or the occult, he or she may find it uncomfortable to disclose the width and breadth of his or her spiritual explorations. When clients move into uncomfortable spaces, spiritual guides can responsibly accompany them by remaining supportive in the session, and doing their homework outside of it.

Just as people frequently move from one faith tradition to another, directors will find that a similar fluidity between the modes of interfaith spiritual direction can be very useful indeed. It may be obvious at a first meeting which mode is appropriate for a particular client, but it is very likely that as the client grows and changes, the mode of interfaith work will change as well.

Spiritual guides will undoubtedly find that they feel more comfortable with one of the modes than the other two, but flexibility as to which mode to use will be rewarded, especially as the needs of each client are unique.

Those who work with groups will find the modes helpful as well, especially as a group is trying to discover who it is and what it seeks to accomplish. Mode II is inappropriate for group work, as the subjective demands are too great, but Modes I and III both work well with groups, and it may be that the group will make a conscious decision about which mode they choose to work in.

Although everyone will have his or her favorite way of working, we should be cautious not to value one mode of interfaith spiritual guidance over others. My own favorite mode to work in is Mode II, but it is obviously inappropriate for most of my clients. Mode III is not the goal, any more than Mode I should be thought of as transitional. Each mode has its proper place in interfaith work, and, no doubt, other models will emerge with time. Interfaith spiritual guidance may be fairly new in the history of the ministry, and it will still seem a novelty to some, but it is quickly becoming the normative model.

The Future of Interfaith Ministry

Interfaith work is still in its infancy. In the past, almost all interfaith work was conducted according to the model described in Mode I—people of different faiths talking and listening to each other from the perspectives of their particular traditions. Yet many interfaith ministers, spiritual guides, and training programs (such as the Chaplaincy Institute for Arts and Interfaith Ministry in Berkeley, California) are embracing a Mode III approach, honoring the wisdom of all traditions, yet being bound to none of them. Such interfaith ministers who work as hospital chaplains can, with appropriate training, effectively minister to anyone who walks through the door. Likewise, spiritual guides who draw from the wisdom of all traditions can provide meaningful companionship to a wide variety of people who seek them out.

Like Guru Nanak, such an approach affirms people in their own tradi-

tions and spiritualities, speaks prophetically to the myopia that entrench-
ment in any one religion can bring, and provides the distance and perspective necessary to see how a tradition has an impact on a client's spiritual life
in both positive and negative ways.

Such an interfaith perspective is not an aberration, but the mere tip of an
iceberg yet to be revealed. In a world divided by ideology, politics, and yes,
religion, the interfaith vision of Nanak calls us to rise above the spiritually
proprietary stance of traditional religion, and to embrace the Divinity that
is the inheritance of every people, regardless of the clothes in which they
dress it.

10

Humanism and the Sacredness of the Mundane

In the preceding chapters, we have given a lot of attention to the various ways people believe, but what about those people who do not—or cannot—believe? Aren't they at times also in need of spiritual guidance? Although I'm sure there are lots of "unbelievers" who would answer that question with a rousing "no!" the truth is that, yes, even those who do not believe in ways recognizable to us are coming for spiritual guidance. How are we to assist them? Should we simply turn them away, or is there a way of understanding their perspective that will help us companion them effectively?

A History of Unbelief

The phenomenon of unbelief goes back a very long way. As early as 1000 B.C.E., a skeptical Indian priest penned a creation hymn utterly unlike anything that had gone before. He wrote, "Who knows for certain? Who shall declare it here? Where did this creation come from, and from what was it born? The gods were born after the creation of the world, so who can know where it came from? No one knows where it came from or who made it. Only the One who beholds it from the highest heaven knows—or maybe he doesn't, and is glad of it."

This poem from the Rig Veda is markedly different from other creation stories in early Hinduism, or indeed, any religion. Instead of telling us where things come from, the writer very honestly admits his ignorance. Many others, who also for reasons of conscience could not embrace the prevailing orthodoxies in their societies, would follow suit.

The skeptical strain in Hinduism is a strong one, for the first avowed agnostic was the Hindu reformer we know as the Budddha. We have already discussed his story at length, but for our purposes here, it is important to point out one of his most innovative teachings: we do not know if there are gods or not, and what's more, it doesn't matter. The gods, for the Buddha, were simply irrelevant. His technique could help someone achieve enlightenment whether one believed in the gods or not.

In the West, the oldest evidence we have of such skepticism is found in the writings of Epicurus, who taught in Greece in the third century B.C.E. Epicurus advanced a kind of materialism, stating that nothing but matter exists. Therefore, when one died, one simply died—there was no spiritual entity that survived the physical body. Meaning, for Epicurus, was found in making the most of what we actually have—enjoying this one life to the fullest. But this was not a mindless hedonism; Epicurus was very clear that moderation was key to a person's prolonged enjoyment of life.

Although Epicurus did not rule out the possibility of some sort of divinity, he certainly struggled with the idea, especially as regards the problem of evil and suffering in the world. He once wrote, "Is God willing to prevent evil, but not able? Then he is not omnipotent. Is he able, but not willing? Then he is malevolent. Is he both able and willing? Then whence cometh evil? Is he neither able nor willing? Then why call him God?"

Epicurus's questions still resonate with philosophers, theologians, and sincere seekers today. All too often, religious folks have simply dismissed this sort of inquiry as being hostile to the spiritual life, but I believe this is a mistake. The spiritual quest should be nothing if not honest, and such questions haunt both believer and unbeliever alike.

Both the Buddha and Epicurus might be called "agnostics" today. The word "agnostic" literally means "not knowing," and identifies a very sincere and humble approach to the Big Questions. Robert Ingersoll, in the nineteenth century, defined the position eloquently:

> Let us be honest with ourselves. In the presence of countless mysteries; standing beneath the boundless heaven sown thick with constellations; knowing that each grain of sand, each leaf, each

blade of grass, asks of every mind the answerless question; knowing that the simplest thing defies solution; feeling that we deal with the superficial and the relative, and that we are forever eluded by the real, the absolute—let us admit the limitations of our minds, and let us have the courage and the candor to say: We do not know.[28]

Agnosticism is a highly respectable and imminently defensible position. While religious believers of every stripe point to their scriptures, mythologies, and traditions with certainty, the agnostic simply shrugs his shoulders and, like the Vedic priest, says "Who knows?" An agnostic cannot in good conscience "pretend" to believe something he or she does not. As there is no scientific, empirical evidence of the existence of God, how can an honest person make an investment in the claims of any religion?

Some skeptics have gone further, however. Unlike the Buddha, who refused to speculate as to the gods' existence or nonexistence, other Hindu reform movements did. Jainism, which is in many ways very similar to Buddhism, openly denied the existence of any deities whatsoever. So did the Hindu Carvaka movement, the primary scripture of which is the Brhaspati Sutra, which was written about 600 B.C.E. Unfortunately, this ancient work has been lost (or, no doubt, destroyed by more theistic Hindus). There are lots of references to the movement, however, even in such august scriptures as the Puranas and the *Bhagavad Gita*, so scholars have been able to piece together many of their teachings.

Their primary doctrine is called *lokayata*, which affirms only the existence of the material world, denies any afterlife, and acknowledges as real only those things that can be perceived.[29] One of their surviving writings, the Sarvasiddhantasamgraha, pulls no punches when it says, "There is no world other than this; there is no Heaven and no Hell; the realm of Shiva and like regions are invented by stupid imposters of other schools of thought."[30]

Today, we would call those who take such positions "atheists." An atheist is someone with a deep conviction that there are no gods. Ironically, Christians were one of the first groups to be called by this term. It is found in ancient Roman writings to refer to those pesky Jesus followers who refused to sacrifice to the state gods. Because they did not acknowledge the Roman pantheon, they were "a-theist," or "against the gods."

Although, as we have seen, it has a long history in the East, atheism as a philosophical position or an ideological movement is a much more recent phenomenon in the West. It only really comes into its own in the nineteenth century. Thomas Paine, one of America's founding fathers, was a deeply committed atheist. He wrote:

> All national institutions of churches, whether Jewish, Christian, or [Muslim], appear to me no other than human inventions set up to terrify and enslave mankind, and monopolize power and profit. . . . I do not mean by this declaration to condemn those who believe otherwise; they have the same right to their belief as I have to mine. But it is necessary to the happiness of man, that he be mentally faithful to himself. Infidelity does not consist in believing, or in disbelieving; it consists in professing to believe what he does not believe.

One of the most interesting and colorful figures in the history of atheism is Charles Bradlaugh, who won his place in the British House of Commons not once, but six times, yet each time he was refused his seat because he would not swear allegiance before God. His situation made him quite a celebrity, and he was, eventually, allowed to take his place in Parliament, but not before bringing considerable attention to the cause of atheism.

Atheism is a more problematic position for a skeptic to take than agnosticism, since it involves a variety of faith. It is, in fact, a form of fundamentalism. Just as the religious fundamentalist says, "I know for certain there is a God," the atheist counters with an equally sincere, "I know for certain there is no God." They are opposite sides of the same coin, though each would no doubt be horrified at the notion.

Most people who proclaim, "I am an atheist" today, are actually more likely to be agnostics. They may be less familiar with the term "agnostic" and often will use the word "atheist" as a catchall phrase referring to any position skeptical of religious orthodoxy. When the distinctions are made clear, most will admit their position is softer (and more rational) than that of the true atheist.

Humanism

While agnostics and atheists define themselves by what they do not believe, humanists understand themselves in terms of what they can affirm.

The former categories depend upon organized religion and are, at their foundations, reactions to such orthodoxies, while humanism seeks to understand itself on its own terms.

Having its foundations in the enlightenment, humanists such as Leonardo da Vinci, John Milton, and Erasmus valued reason and reverence for life over blind obedience to religious authority. Often persecuted for thinking critically about religion in public, these early humanists courageously blazed an ideological trail that would eventually become a spirituality in its own right. While these early humanists were believers, after their own fashion, and sought a more reasonable approach to their own faiths, the values they espoused provided a guiding light for those who came after them, who were increasingly critical toward matters of religion and faith.

Humanists believe that it is possible to define morality apart from religious standards. Ethics, for humanists, derive from human reason, lived experience, and the conscious cultivation of compassion. Humanists do not seek to behave ethically out of fear of divine retribution (which they consider a childish motivation), but simply because, logically, empathetically, it is the right thing to do. While this may seem at first glance to be a dangerously subjective criterion for human behavior, it must be pointed out that religiously motivated morality has often been capricious and cruel by contemporary reckoning. A rational and consistent attempt to define morality cannot be a bad thing, given religion's spotty track record.

Humanists affirm that all people have basic human rights, as well as ethical responsibilities toward society and the natural world. They affirm that human beings have all the tools they need at hand to solve persistent problems in the world such as hunger, warfare, prejudice, and environmental destruction. Too often, however, the obstacles to these much-needed solutions are religious in origin: "tribal" rivalries objectify those not like us and demonize other cultures and beliefs; puritanical religious mores shun and demean sexual minorities, those women who are pregnant out of wedlock, and divorced persons; and eschatological anticipation has led to an outright dismissal of ecological responsibility.

One should not make the mistake of assuming that all of this blessed rationality is utterly void of spirituality, however. Humanists may or may not believe in the existence of the soul, though those that do are not likely to understand it in terms recognizable to any established orthodoxy. But spirituality, for humanists, has far less to do with the afterlife or nonembodied existence, and everything to do with quality of life here on earth. Such qualities as empathy, beauty, truth, connection, reverence, depth, meaning, and feeling are qualities common to all humankind, and provide the basis for a rich interior life—a soulful life, if you will—not dependent upon the affirmation of any supernatural "realities."

Humanists may appreciate scriptures and sacred texts for their insight into the human experience, but will do so without appropriating the dogma of the traditions they hail from. In addition, they will give equal weight to every sort of literature, music, art, and film that touches us at the core of our beings, instructs us, and makes us better people. All cultural and artistic expressions offer insight into what it means to be human, and this, for humanists, is truly sacred.

Humanists may even be described as possessing a profound mysticism, one that affirms the human being as fully and completely part of this universe. When a humanist looks out at the stars and recognizes that the gooseflesh rising on her arms had its origin in the Big Bang and is as old as the most distant galaxy, it fosters a rich feeling of belonging, of cosmic kinship with all of being that rivals any religious emotion. We are all "starstuff," we are all one thing with many expressions, we will all rise and fall and rise again in a new form. To enter into this mystery willingly, consciously, unhindered by superstition or fear of divine wrath is a mystical orientation indeed.

The "moral compass" for humanists, then, is not pointing toward any otherworldly reality—not toward the promise or threat of Heaven or Hell, not toward any deity, horrific or benign. Instead, it points persistently toward the earth itself, toward the well-being of its creatures, toward equality and freedom for all peoples. A more noble—even religious—goal will be hard to find.

It is no surprise then, that humanists, like anyone else with a rich interior life, may seek a more intentional expression of their spirituality. When Sally wrote me and asked me to companion her via e-mail, she did so because she had read many of my sermons online, and trusted that, although I was a Christian minister, I would not take the easy way out by appealing to faith as she wrestled with her issues. I was grateful for her trust, and though I have, now and then, caught myself sliding into the "realm of faith," she has been very good at keeping my nose to the grindstone.

An artistic liberal living in the Bible Belt, Sally had tried being a Christian for a while, but had felt inauthentic doing so. She finally had given up on organized forms of religion and any conventional notion of the Divine. Yet she was also troubled by growing older and the fact of her own impending death seemed to mock her. It all seemed so pointless, so arbitrary. She also struggled with being childless, knowing that when her life ended it would simply end without the benefit of children carrying on her genetic legacy.

Yet Sally also found herself deeply moved by music and poetry, though she found it difficult to articulate exactly why this was. To what do such transcendent experiences point? How could she find adequate meaning in a life of finite duration?

In guiding such people, I consider myself to be less a spiritual guide and more of an existential coach. There is much in Sally's spiritual dilemma that I relate to, and I have felt deeply privileged to have walked with her via e-mail for over four years, now. After all this time, Sally has found few answers to her questions, but she has found the relationship we share valuable as it has provided safe space for her to ask the big questions, to wrestle with the elusive specter of divinity, and to sit with both despair and elation.

There are many Sallys in the world, people who cannot embrace religiosity, yet who cannot escape the fundamental human conditions of decay and death, and struggle to find meaning in the midst of it. The degree to which we can resist the temptation to resort to the answers provided by dogma and faith and simply be *with* people in their painful unknowing will be the degree to which we can be effective spiritual guides for atheists, agnostics, and humanists.

The Sacredness of the Ordinary

For humanist clients, meaning must be found in this world, or in none. Morality and ethics must be grounded in human experience rather than divine revelation. And instead of looking to another world as the source of transcendence and spiritual experience, such mystical connection is in ample supply in the here and now, if only we have the eyes to see it.

This insight is the gift of humanism to our ministry of spiritual guidance, as there are many aspects of this work that are decidedly mundane. There is little about record keeping, taxes, or marketing that seems to us inherently spiritual, but to deny the sacredness of these "ordinary" activities is to miss an invitation to infuse our daily living with purpose and depth. We may not be goading someone to enlightenment when alone at night balancing our checkbooks, but with reason and compassion as our guides, we would be in error to assume that there is no opportunity for ministry or the cultivation of soulful living in such an activity.

As humanism teaches us, every mundane activity has ethical (or unethical) consequences. How we treat one another, how we share this good earth with our kindred creatures, and how we tend to the earth herself are questions to be addressed in every action. Far from liberating us from moral strictures, humanism imposes upon us an even greater responsibility—for not only must we attend to how we act, we must also *think* about our actions and how their effects ripple out into the universe.

Your faith tradition may have little to say about how you market your practice, but humanism asks many hard questions about it: Who is affected, who offended, who is helped by this or that strategy? Are our motivations selfish, myopic, or truly philanthropic? Humanism asks us to sit with the many complicated implications of our actions—a holy contemplation if there ever was one.

In the balance of this chapter we will look at the more "mundane" aspects of growing and maintaining a private practice in interfaith spiritual guidance, with special emphasis on how to tend to such matters with reason and compassion for the wider web of being of which we are a part.

Providing a Hospitable Space

As we have already learned, spiritual guidance is primarily a ministry of hospitality. In sitting with clients we are holding a welcoming space for both them and the Divine. In preparing such a space, there are important concerns to be considered. Is the space clean and inviting? Is it dark and dingy, or is it well lit and well aired? If the room is messy or a wreck, it may not be a place where your client will want to spend much time. Also pay close attention to the plants in your room—if they are not well tended, it may send the wrong kind of message about the sort of attention your clients might expect to receive, as well.

When I first starting seeing clients in my church office, I was perplexed by the yellowed walls, the salmon shag carpet (all the rage in the '70s) and the stacks of paper that had accumulated over the years—old bulletins, flyers, and theme sheets that no one had the heart to toss. The chief offender, however, was the dingy couch left over from the Eisenhower administration. It was threadbare, one leg was missing, and, quite frankly, it stank to high heaven. In addition, sitting in it was like quicksand—it provided no support; and if not careful, one could not extract one's self without aid from fellow adventurers.

With permission from our Board of Trustees, and with help from a willing parishioner, we tossed out all the paper, painted the walls, replaced the carpet, and cast the couch into the outer darkness (rather, we had it hauled to the dump). Two new, comfy chairs from Ikea and some tasteful artwork transformed the room into a place where people actually look forward to spending some time.

Your space should be viewed just as critically: how would you feel if you were a guest, spending an hour in this space? If you are too familiar with the place you may not be able to evaluate it critically. If so, enlist the aid of a friend—preferably one with some taste.

Many people see clients in their own homes, but this comes with its own set of problems. This works best if you have a dedicated room that can be accessed independently from the outside. Even if your dedicated room can be kept clean, do people have to walk through a messy house to reach it? If so, this will serve to undermine the sense of well-being, security, and peace that you are trying to establish.

You may be able to rent a room from your church for this purpose, or you may want to band together with other spiritual guides and rent a therapist's office. If there are seven of you, and you each see clients one day per week, such an arrangement might be ideal. The cost will be minimal, but the professional appearance of your office will inspire confidence and establish the welcoming spirit you are trying to evoke.

Decorating your space comes with its own set of challenges. If you are fond of religious icons, will they make some clients uncomfortable? For instance, if your own faith tradition is Buddhism, and your icons are all Tibetan *tankas*, will your Jewish client find the space alienating? If you have a variety of religious symbols from many traditions, will it frighten the Baptist woman just beginning to experiment with spiritual guidance?

Everyone must answer these questions for him- or herself, but attention to such details is important. They are mundane and seemingly unimportant things, yet proper attention to them may significantly impact the degree to which your clients feel welcome, and whether they will feel safe to divulge their souls. There is nothing "spiritual" about decorating a room, but attention to how such decor will affect your clients is a sacred concern nonetheless.[31]

Paperwork

Though spiritual guidance is a ministry that consists of mostly sitting and listening to people, there is also a bit of paperwork to tend to. Not much, thankfully, but important, nonetheless.

Covenants. First there is the matter of a covenant, or a written agreement between the spiritual guide and the client, which we mentioned briefly in chapter five. This covenant is important in that it describes, up front, what your client can expect from you, and what you require of your client. Such a document might contain a definition of spiritual guidance as you understand it, and a bit about your training and commitment to ongoing education in your field. It should definitely spell out what your client can expect in the way of confidentiality, including situations in which such privilege may be revoked. The document should spell out your fees, duration of the session, and what you expect if an appointment is missed. An example of such a form is found in appendix B, and is adapted for interfaith use from a version used by the Bread of Life Center in Davis, California.

This document should be presented at the first meeting with a client, and might be signed then and there, or the client may wish to take it home for more careful consideration, and bring it to the second session. Using such a document is a way of showing respect for your client, for clear communication, and for yourself and your ministry. It communicates the professional nature of the relationship to your client, and helps get things "off on the right foot."

Notes. No matter how good your memory is, you must always keep notes on your clients and each individual session. This is useful in preparing for a session in that you can review your notes of the last session to "catch you up," to remind yourself of the content of the last session, whatever homework you might have assigned to the client, and feelings, thoughts, and nudges you may have had but did not have time to follow up on.

You must also keep notes for legal reasons. If, for instance, you have a client who is involved in a criminal trial, or is going through a divorce, your records may be subpoenaed by a court of law. Your notes may be required as evidence. Of course, out of regard for confidentiality, you may refuse, and you may go to jail for a short time because of it. This is between you, your client, and the Divine. But in case it is actually in your client's best interest, you may (with his or her permission) actually *need* to surrender your notes. And in the case that you are sued for malpractice by a client, you had better pray that your notes are complete, in order, and intact.

If you are working for a retreat center or another organization, your session notes are the property of the institution. If you are in private practice, they are yours. Ultimately, however, they belong to the client, and the client may ask to see your notes at any time—a request that you cannot legally refuse. So be careful to keep your notes on-topic, and keep the editorial comments (such as, "What a numbskull!") to a minimum.

Some people will take ten minutes after a session to jot down the main points covered in a session. I myself prefer to take notes on a clipboard throughout each session (I have a lousy memory). This is a matter of preference, and each spiritual guide will need to decide for him- or herself what will work best. I like having paper and pen handy in case nudgings come in the midst of a session that I cannot address at the moment, but will want to return to. I also like having a place I can write the random things that occur to me during a session that have no bearing on the client but that I do not want to forget, so I can let go of it and be more fully present. For instance, jotting down "dry cleaning" will remind me to pick up my dry cleaning on the way home. It's much better to take three seconds to scribble such a note and then dismiss it than to obsess about it and be distracted.

Keeping notes communicates to your client that you value your sessions together, that important work is being done, and that there is a record of it. Thus it is not only helpful for you, it is legally necessary, and displays respect for the client. Sure, it's a pain, and there's nothing supernatural or transcendent about it, but few things are more helpful in tending to your client.

Taxes. If you make more than $400 per year from your spiritual guidance, you will need to pay taxes. Figuring out how much you took in at the end of the year is easy if you have noted how much your clients paid you in your session notes. I always put the amount tendered in the top right hand corner of each sheet of session notes. This allows me to breeze through my files, rather than having to search through the notes or my checkbook for the information. If your office has a copy machine handy, you may also wish to photocopy each check you receive, and just place it in your client's file.

Liz Stout's wonderful article, "Building Your Practice of Spiritual Direction," recommends a number of items that may be deductible from your taxes: rent for office space, telephone or fax lines, custodial services, furniture, door locks, business cards and other promotional items, postage used, classes, conferences, retreats, educational materials (books and magazines related to your practice), insurance, professional organization dues, and mileage. If you keep your receipts in order, it could actually amount to more than you expect. Since self-employment taxes are steep, it is wise to be meticulous in this area.

Reporting taxes should be a priority as it is part of our covenant with our community. There may not be any religious dimension to it, but ethical behavior, as we have seen, does not require a divine mandate. Keeping faith with clients, with the government, and with our own integrity should not *be* a matter of faith, but of conscience.

Insurance. It used to be that the notion of needing malpractice insurance for spiritual guidance was laughable—no more. Though lawsuits against spiritual guides are rare, they are more common than they used to be, and it is foolish to dismiss the possibility. Ours is an extremely litigious culture, and people are likely to sue whenever they are unhappy. Even the most gifted spiritual guides inadvertently antagonize people now and then—you will be no different. Should one of those disgruntled souls decide to air his or her grievances against you before a court of law, you will be grateful if you have some insurance backing you up (especially if you are fond of your house).

Insurance for spiritual guides used to be nearly impossible to get. It was, for a long time, the Holy Grail of the guidance community—everyone wanted it, but nobody knew where to find it. Fortunately, our ministry is finally catching up with the times in this regard. Joining Spiritual Directors International is a good idea for a number of reasons. For our purposes here, it is the only surefire way of gaining insurance for those guides who cannot gain insurance through a related practice (such as psychotherapists or clergy). SDI, through a special arrangement with the American Professional Agency, now offers malpractice insurance for about $100 per year—a bargain indeed.

Don't let the forms you need to fill out scare you off—they list us as "mental health professionals." Whatever—they have to shoehorn us into their system in a way that makes sense to them, even if it makes no sense to us. It's obvious that the insurance and legal industries are still in need of some education on the ministry of spiritual guidance. Yet the fact that we can now be insured, where only a couple of years ago we could not, is progress indeed, and worthy of celebration.

Sure, it sounds like a commercial: "Insurance—don't do spiritual guidance without it," but it's true. Before you see that first client, get that coverage. You will not be sorry, and you'll sleep easier at night.

Marketing and Networking

Once you have all the basics down and you have your space, you are ready to receive clients. But where will this elusive species come from? Although twenty years ago spiritual guides would have shuddered at the idea of marketing, today it is simply unavoidable if you are in private practice.

The best way to gather clients is by word of mouth. It involves the least amount of overt salesmanship, but still takes some work nonetheless. Clients who love working with you will refer others to you—but this is a catch-22, as you must have clients in the first place to do the referring. The best source of referrals is other spiritual guides.

Membership in Spiritual Directors International offers an invaluable networking opportunity. SDI is divided into many local regions, many of which host their own activities. Some get together monthly to socialize, swap ideas, hear a speaker (and thus further their education), and, yes, *network*. Once other spiritual guides get to know you, like you, *trust* you, they will refer clients to you when it seems to them a good fit.

As Liz Stout points out, one good way to distinguish yourself is to make people you network with aware of your specialties. For instance, I specialize in working with people in recovery from religious abuse, Generation X, and people from alternative religious traditions. So, when someone in my area hears of a thirty-something Wiccan who grew up Fundamentalist, my name is likely to come up. Your familiarity with distinctive populations will be your biggest networking ally.

Other networking opportunities are out there, as well. Gatherings of other helping professionals are also excellent places to get word of your ministry out. In a meeting of your local interfaith clergy council or a social for transpersonal psychologists, the uniqueness of your ministry will make you stand out. People will remember you, and when they come across someone who fits your profession better than theirs, may send them along to you.

Public speaking and writing are also excellent marketing tools. If you give lectures on spiritual guidance at local synagogues and churches, you may pick up a client or two from among your listeners. Or you may find that once your audience has gone home and talked with their friends about what they heard, their friends or friends of friends may call you.

If you teach classes in religion or a related field, students may seek you out as a spiritual guide for them. You may also want to organize spiritual direction groups. Most of these are free, but the time is well invested if, after the group has finished its work, one or two of the group members continue with you in individual sessions.

Suggesting or writing an article on spiritual guidance for a local newspaper has yielded great results for some guides. This also works for newsletters, house organs, and magazines. Sometimes just listing your status as a professional spiritual guide in your biography at the end of an article completely unrelated to spiritual guidance will have curious folks sending you some e-mails to learn more.

Depending on how web-savvy you are, a website might be an excellent tool. A friend and I put up a website about five years ago hoping to drum up some spiritual guidance and wedding business. Once it was indexed by the various web crawlers, it popped up whenever someone googled "bay area" and "weddings" or "spiritual direction." I still get at least one spiritual guidance client or wedding a year from that site, even though I haven't touched it in five years, or marketed the site in any way.

A well-placed flyer at bookstores, houses of worship, coffee shops, and schools may also yield some results, especially if the flyer is well designed and inviting. And business cards are never a bad idea—they can be tacked in the smallest spaces on almost any bulletin board.

Some spiritual guides, especially those trained in traditional contexts, may object to the idea of marketing your ministry. What has Spirit to do with the marketplace after all? It may seem to them tacky, ill-advised, even blasphemous. Yet the truth is, the world is different than it was twenty years ago. Although many spiritual guides worked in the past for retreat centers, where clients came specifically for spiritual care; most guides these days are freelancers—private practitioners—and clients must come from somewhere.

Conclusion

The idea that spirit and matter (or mammon) do not mix is a false dualism based on a romantic notion we can no longer afford to countenance—the world has moved on, even if our religious traditions have not. The sacred and secular are not two completely separate spheres of existence, and we try to separate them at our peril if we want to establish thriving practices. Religion, after all, is bigger business than ever it was before, and business is giving more attention to the Spirit, as well. Spiritual guidance is both a ministry and a business, and, as humanism has shown us, the mundane side of things is no less worthy of soulful attention than the spiritual. Approaching the nitty-gritty details of our practice with ethical devotion, compassion, and mindfulness creates a spiritual foundation that supports and informs the rest of our practice. Far from being "unspiritual," how we approach this "shadow" side of our ministry casts light upon every other aspect of the practice.

Appendix A

Spiritual Directors International
Guidelines for Ethical Conduct

Ethical conduct flows from lived reverence for Divinity, self, and others but is not inevitably the reality of every spiritual direction relationship. Therefore, these guidelines are meant to inspire members of Spiritual Directors International toward integrity, responsibility, and faithfulness in their practice of spiritual direction.

I. The Spiritual Director and the Self

1. Personal Spirituality. Spiritual directors assume responsibility for personal growth by: a) participating in regular spiritual direction; b) following personal and communal spiritual practices and disciplines.

2. Formation. Spiritual directors engage in ongoing formation as directors by: a) continuing to discern their call to the ministry of spiritual direction; b) nurturing self-knowledge and freedom; c) cultivating insight into the influences of culture, social-historical context, environmental setting, and institutions; d) studying scripture, theology, spirituality, and other disciplines related to spiritual direction.

3. Supervision. Spiritual directors engage in supervision by a) receiving regular supervision from peers or from a mentor; b) seeking consultations with other appropriately qualified persons when necessary.

4. Personal Responsibility. Spiritual directors meet their needs outside the spiritual direction relationship in a variety of ways, especially by: a) self care, wisely balancing time for worship, work, leisure, family, and personal relationships; b) addressing the difficulties multiple roles or relationships pose to the effectiveness or clarity of the spiritual direction relationship; c) removing oneself from any situation that compromises the integrity of the spiritual direction relationship.

5. Limitations. Spiritual directors recognize the limits of: a) energy by restricting the number of directees; b) attentiveness by appropriate spacing of meetings and directees; c) competence by referring directees to other appropriately qualified persons when necessary.

II. The Spiritual Director and the Directee

1. Covenant. Spiritual directors initiate conversation and establish agreements with directees about: a) the nature of spiritual direction; b) the roles of the director and the directee; c) the length and frequency of direction sessions; d) the compensation, if any, to be given to the director or institution; e) the process for evaluating and terminating the relationship.

2. Dignity. Spiritual directors honor the dignity of the directee by: a) respecting the directee's values, conscience, spirituality, and theology; b) inquiring into the motives, experiences, or relationships of the directee only as necessary; c) recognizing the imbalance of power in the spiritual direction relationship and taking care not to exploit it; d) establishing and maintaining appropriate physical and psychological boundaries with the directee; e) refraining from sexualized behavior, including, but not limited to, manipulative, abusive, or coercive words or actions toward a directee.

3. Confidentiality. Spiritual directors maintain the confidentiality and the privacy of the directee by: a) protecting the identity of the directee; b) keeping confidential all oral and written matters arising in the spiritual direction sessions; c) conducting direction sessions in appropriate settings; d) addressing legal regulations requiring disclosure to proper authorities, including but not limited to, child abuse, elder abuse, and physical harm to self and others.

III. The Spiritual Director and Others

1. Colleagues. Spiritual directors maintain collegial relationships with ministers and professionals by: a) developing intra- and interdisciplinary relationships; b) requesting a directee who is in therapy to inform his or her therapist about being in spiritual direction; c) securing written releases and permission from directees when specific information needs to be shared for the benefit of the directee; d) respecting ministers and professionals by not disparaging them or their work.

2. *Faith Communities*. Spiritual directors maintain responsible relationships to communities of faith by: a) remaining open to processes of corporate discernment, accountability, and support; b) appropriately drawing on the teachings and practices of communities of faith; c) respecting the directee's relationship to his or her own community of faith.

3. *Society*. Spiritual directors, when presenting themselves to the public, preserve the integrity of spiritual direction by: a) representing qualifications and affiliations accurately; b) defining the particular nature and purpose of spiritual direction; c) respecting all persons regardless of race, color, sex, sexual orientation, age, religion, national origin, marital status, political belief, mental or physical handicap, any preference, personal characteristic, condition, or status.

Appendix B
Spiritual Guidance Statement of Policy

Adapted for interfaith use from the Statement
used by the Bread of Life Center in Davis, CA.

The Nature of Spiritual Guidance

Spiritual guidance is a process that focuses on conscious development of one's human potential and/or growing the relationship between a person and the Divine. This can happen in either one-to-one sessions or in small group settings. The guide helps a person notice and respond to the unfolding universe of which we are all a part, and to connect with the larger community of being. This might include helping someone learn to meditate or pray, providing support for discernment and decision-making, and becoming aware of feelings and images which may be nudging one towards wholeness. Although it is not a counseling or therapeutic relationship, many find spiritual guidance a helpful companion process to work happening in these other settings.

What You Can Expect from a Spiritual Guide

All of our guides have been trained in recognized programs that follow the guiding principles and components of *Spiritual Directors International*. These components include theological and psychological dimensions of direction, discernment, practicum, and supervision. We have adopted for ourselves the proposed ethical guidelines of this association. We commit to our own personal growth by seeking monthly spiritual guidance ourselves and by active participation in a community of faith. We commit to our ongoing professional growth by attending at least one continuing education event in the field each year, and by participating monthly in a supervision process.

Confidentiality

To assure the best quality of care for those who come to us, our guides may consult with one another or with another professional. Any information shared in supervision or consultation is anonymous and held in strictest confidence. Outside of these settings nothing is shared without your written consent, except as required by law to protect you or another from serious harm. Your director is required by law to report known or suspected cases of abuse or neglect to children, the elderly, and the handicapped.

Fees and Payment

Standard fees are $50 per individual session. Our desire is that no one be limited by finances and so a sliding scale is available. Your guide will be happy to discuss your particular situation. Group spiritual guidance is also available with fees dependent on the size of the group. Because a billing system would add cost we ask that you pay at the time of service.

Appointments

Regular meetings are essential to effective guidance, and are negotiated between the client and spiritual guide. Once the relationship is established, a typical rhythm for meeting is once a month for 50 minutes. The time set aside by you and your guide is your reserved time. If you are unable to keep your appointment, please call at least 24 hours in advance and ask to be rescheduled. You are responsible for paying the fee for your appointment if you do not call and cancel 24 hours in advance, with exceptions being sudden illness and situations over which you have no control.

I have read and understand this policy statement and agree with it.
(Please sign and take a copy for your records.)

Signature: _____   Date: _____

Appendix C

Authorization of Release of Information

By signing this document, I, _____,

(hereinafter "Client") hereby authorize _____

(the spiritual guide) to disclose confidential spiritual guidance information

and records to: Name and/or Organization _____

_____

Role _____

Telephone Number_____

I understand that I have a right to receive a copy of this authorization.
I understand that any cancellation or modification of this authorization must be in writing. I understand that I have the right to revoke
this authorization at any time unless_____(the
spiritual guide) has taken action in reliance upon it. And, I also understand
that such revocation must be in writing and received by_____
_____ (the spiritual guide) to be effective.

This disclosure of information and records authorized by Client is required for the following purpose:

_____

_____

The specific uses and limitations on the types of medical information to be discussed are as follows:

_____

_____

Such disclosure shall be limited to the following specific types of information:

_____

_____

Client has the right to refuse to sign this form.

Client understands that information used or disclosed pursuant to this authorization may be subject to re-disclosure by the recipient and may no longer be protected by the Federal Privacy Rule, although such information may be protected by applicable state law.

This authorization shall remain valid until:_____

Client:_____Date: _____

Notes

Chapter 1

1. I am indebted to Wayne Swindall for this illustration.
2. This approach is covered very well in Mary Ann Dougherty's classic *Group Spiritual Direction* (New York: Paulist Press, 1995).
3. This model is described in *Wisdom Circles* by Charles Garfield, Cindy Spring, and Sedonia Cahill (New York: Hyperion, 1998).
4. "Brief Encounters: What Spiritual Directors Can Learn from the Short-Term Therapy Model," in *Presence* (October 2002).

Chapter 2

5. John Mabry, *Tao Te Ching: A New Version* (Berkeley, CA: Apocryphile Press, 2004).
6. *The Complete Works of Chuang Tzu*, translated by Burton Watson (New York: Columbia University Press, 1968), 73.
7. Ibid., 188.
8. *The Hidden Ground of Love: Letters* by Thomas Merton; edited by William H. Shannon (New York: Farrar, Straus, Giroux, 1985), 627.
9. *Meditations with Mechtilde of Magdeburg . . .* by Sue Woodruff (Santa Fe: Bear & Co., 1982).

Chapter 3

10. Adapted from *The Power of Myth* by Joseph Campbell with Bill Moyers, edited by Betty Sue Flowers (New York: Doubleday, 1988).
11. See Huston Smith, *The World's Religions* (New York: HarperCollins, 1991), 32–50.
12. *Hymns for the Drowning: Poems for Vishnu by Nammalvar*, translated by A.K. Ramanujan (Princeton, NJ: Princeton University Press, 1981), p 68.
13. "To Bring All Things Together: Spiritual Direction As Action for Justice," printed in *Presence*, January 1995. Keegan acknowledges that the system he describes is a synthesis of two systems, called "The Grid" and the "Experience Cycle" (developed at the Center for Spirituality and Justice in New Rochelle, NY) and compiled by his colleague Steve Wirth with input from Elinor Shea; Jack Mostyn, CFC; Peter M. Senge; and Chris Argyris.

Chapter 4

14. "The Compassionate Observer," *Presence*, September 1998.
15. Ibid., 25; italics mine.
16. Ibid.

Chapter 5
17. See Exodus 32:14 for just one example.
18. Since this name is too holy to speak aloud, the Jews substitute the word "Adonai," which is Hebrew for "the Lord."

Chapter 6
19. *Soul Retrieval: Mending the Fragmented Self* by Sandra Ingerman (San Francisco: HarperSanFrancisco, 1991).
20. For more on the Urim and Thummim, see Exodus 28:30, Leviticus 8:8, Numbers 27:21, Deuteronomy 33:8, 1 Samuel 28:6, Ezra 2:63, and Nehemiah 7:65.
21. *Choice Centered Tarot* by Gail Fairfield (North Hollywood: Newcastle Publishing, 1984).

Chapter 7
22. Gospel of Thomas, 113.
23. Adapted for inclusive language from the New American Standard Version (The Lockman Foundation).
24. Regina Baümer and Michael Plattig, "Desert Fathers and Spiritual Direction," in *Presence* (Summer 2001).

Chapter 9
25. *The Name of My Beloved: Verses of the Sikh Gurus*, translated by Nikky-Guninder Kaur Singh (San Francisco: HarperSanFrancisco, 1995), 18.
26. *The Joy of Sects* by Peter Occhiogrosso (New York: Doubeday, 1994), 57.
27. *Beloved*, 17–18.

Chapter 10
28. For the information on the history of atheism and humanism, I am indebted to anonymous articles posted on the following websites:
www.objectivethought.com/atheism/history.html
www.bbc.co.uk/religion/religions/atheism/history/
29. See *A Sourcebook in Indian Philosophy* by Sarvepalli Radhakrishnan and Charles A. Moore (Princeton, NJ: Princeton University Press, 1957) for more on this movement.
30. Ibid., 235.
31. For inspiration on the practical aspects of private practice, I am indebted to Elizabeth G. Stout's article "Building Your Practice of Spiritual Direction," (*Presence*, January 2001) and Robert J. Willis's "Professionalism, Legal Responsibilities, and Record Keeping," (*Presence*, January 1995).